AFRICAN SOCIETY TODAY

Migrant Laborers

Migrant Laborers surveys the large literature on labor migration in east, west and southern Africa and interprets it from a political economy perspective. It addresses the controversies as to the origins of migrancy and its effects on the rural economy, emphasizing the differences in the response of various African pre-capitalist societies to wage labor, and the regional variations in the effects on the rural economy and on the division of labor within the rural household. Male migrants' experiences with forced labor, recruitment systems, advance payments and compound controls are described, and the rather different character of women's migration is examined.

A central concern is the development of migrant workers' consciousness and forms of resistance. Under what conditions are the labor-market divisions between migrant and non-migrant workers overcome? When do migrants move beyond strategies of desertion and labor mobility to collective on-site work actions such as strikes and unionism? Labor protest among dockers, miners and domestic workers is examined with respect to these questions. Finally, the persistence of migrancy in South Africa today is contrasted to the decline of labor migrancy in other parts of the continent.

AFRICAN SOCIETY TODAY

General editor: ROBIN COHEN

Advisory editors:
O. Aribiah, Jean Copans, Paul Lubeck, Philip M. Mbithi,
M. S. Muntemba, O. Nnoli, Richard Sandbrook

The series has been designed to provide scholarly, but lively and up-to-date, books, likely to appeal to a wide readership. The authors will be drawn from the field of development studies and all the social sciences, and will also have had experience of teaching and research in a number of African countries.

The books will deal with the various social groups and classes that comprise contemporary African society and successive volumes will link with previous volumes to create an integrated and comprehensive picture of the African social structure.

Also in the series

Farm labour. KEN SWINDELL
The politics of Africa's economic stagnation. RICHARD SANDBROOK

MIGRANT LABORERS

∫₂

SHARON STICHTER

CAMBRIDGE UNIVERSITY PRESS
Cambridge
London   New York   New Rochelle
Melbourne   Sydney

Published by the Press Syndicate of the University of Cambridge
The Pitt Building, Trumpington Street, Cambridge CB2 1RP
32 East 57th Street, New York, NY 10022, USA
10 Stamford Road, Oakleigh, Melbourne 3166, Australia

© Cambridge University Press 1985

First published 1985

Printed in Great Britain at the University Press, Cambridge

Library of Congress catalogue card number: 85-4098

British Library Cataloguing in Publication Data

Stichter, Sharon
Migrant laborers. – (African society
today)
1. Migrant labor – Africa
1. Title II. Series
331.5'44'096   HD5856.A/

ISBN 0 521 25118 4 hard covers
ISBN 0 521 27213 0 paperback

CONTENTS

1 Migration and development — page 1
2 Migrants and the rural economy — 29
3 Migration and the African household — 58
4 Entering and leaving the work force — 88
5 Migrants at the work place — 120
6 Women as migrants and workers — 144
7 Migrants, protest and the future — 179

Notes — 196
Index — 221

1

MIGRATION AND DEVELOPMENT

Circular labor migration is not unique to Africa, yet it has been one of the most distinctive features of that continent's development. To understand it, we must grasp not only its general function in early capitalist development, but also those characteristics of Africa which have made it so common a pattern there. Temporary labor migrants shuttle between two different modes of production, capitalist wage employment on the one hand, and some form of pre- or partially capitalist subsistence or peasant production on the other. Return migration is a phenomenon of the incomplete separation of the worker from his or her means of production.

Temporary participation in the labor market involving spatial movement has been common in all parts of the world during early industrial development. Russian lords provided serfs for the textile factories in Moscow in the eighteenth century, allowing them to migrate on a temporary basis.[1] Chinese labor contractors brought hundreds of villagers to the coal- and salt-mines for specified periods of time in the nineteenth and twentieth centuries.[2] Return migration has been important in other parts of Asia and in Latin America.[3] But, as development, whether capitalist or socialist, proceeds, circulatory labor migration tends to decline. From a comparative perspective, the reason that return migration remains so prevalent in Africa has to do with the lack of industrial development. Only one country, South Africa, has successfully industrialized on the basis of enforced migrancy.

In other areas of Africa the low level of industrial development still makes it possible for many enterprises to rely on cheap, less skilled and less stabilized labor. At the same time, the lack of penetration of capital into agriculture has left small-scale peasant and subsistence farming and herding as attainable, although materially not very satisfactory, options for the majority of the population. But when explaining the origins of the migrancy system, as distinct from its continuance, there is reason to argue that conditions specific to African pre-colonial social formations themselves, in addition to external forces, contributed to determining that migrancy would be the predominant form of wage labor for the first half-century of capitalist development.

APPROACHES TO MIGRANTS

The term 'migrant laborer' encompasses a range of patterns of participation in the labor force, but at the same time specifically excludes several other types of migration. More or less permanent migration of whole kin groups has been common in Africa for centuries; movements were often undertaken out of economic necessity, for example to control trade routes or to get access to fertile land for cultivation or grazing. In fact, it was the colonial authorities who by and large attempted to curb these movements, the official view being that Africans ought to have a *permanent* rural home, to which the male could be returned after temporary migration for wage labor, and which could support his family. For this reason forms of migration such as the seasonal movement of pastoralists were discouraged under colonial rule.

A modern version of pre-colonial migration has been brought about by the successful development of African-grown cash crops in some areas, resulting in in-migration. Immigrants often come first as laborers in a typical migrant pattern, but then establish themselves as independent producers and bring in their families. The cotton- and coffee-growing areas of Buganda, the cocoa-producing areas of Ghana, and the palm-oil producing areas of Nigeria are, or have been, areas of extensive in-migration. In 1948, for example, one-third of the population of Buganda consisted of migrants from other parts of Uganda, or from Tanzania, Sudan or Rwanda.[4]

This volume does not deal with these kinds of migration, but focusses exclusively on the temporary migration of individuals into and out of wage employment. We use the term 'labor migrant' to refer specifically to a person who moves between wage work and some other mode of production, over some spatial distance. We do not include those who migrate in order to engage in trade, farming or other self-employment, nor do we include an individual who, upon leaving wage employment, is completely without an income; he or she must have some alternative way of getting an income, usually in the peasant or subsistence economy. In theory, one might include those who, as is so typical in many Third World cities, move periodically between employment and urban self-employment, but this pattern usually does not involve much migration.[5]

Within these parameters, patterns of labor participation can vary widely, from the long-service clerk or miner who brings his family with him to town but still returns to the rural area without pension upon retirement, to the unskilled laborer who works only a few days or weeks before returning home. Between these extremes are many variations, depending in the first instance on length of stay in the labor force. This is not equivalent to length of stay in a particular job; migrants such as those to the central and southern African copper- and gold-mines often move from job to job or have periods of unemployment between jobs. For our purposes it is not job turnover but turnover between wage and non-wage work that is the key factor. Other important variations among workers stem from the distance traveled, whether long or short (each representing a different investment of time and resources), and the degree of dependence on wage work as opposed to other sources of income. Another crucial factor consists in the political–legal terms of the migrant's incorporation into the labor force: whether participation is in one way or another forced (as was common in the early colonial era) or is in some sense voluntary, and also the duration and terms of the contract. We return to the description of the various patterns of participation in Chapter 4. A final differentiating factor among workers is the kinds of familial and pre-capitalist social obligations the migrant is enmeshed in in his or her home area; these too have an impact on the pattern of work and the disposition of wages. They are more fully described in Chapters 2 and 3.

These considerations point to the need for understanding both the political–economic situation from which migrants come, which determines their decision to migrate, or forces them to do so, as well as the situation which they enter as workers, which influences their actions as workers and determines, or in some cases forces, their decision to return home. In Chapters 2 and 3 we look at the experiences of migrants in the rural areas, and in Chapters 4, 5 and 6 we examine the migrant as worker. Throughout, we want to consider not only the question of out-migration, but also that of return migration, that is, the failure of the wage system to absorb workers on a permanent basis. And, most important, we want to examine what actions and reactions have been provoked by Africans' experiences as workers, other than simply their comings and goings. Too often the scholarly work on labor migration has ignored the dimension of labor protest, while the work on labor protest has had difficulty in coming to grips with the impact of migration or temporary proletarianization. In this book we shall emphasize that entering or leaving the labor market can be in itself one of the main responses workers have to the terms and conditions of their employment. At the same time it is only one of a number of kinds of action migrant workers have taken in the struggle for a better living for themselves and their families.

In the scholarly literature on labor migration there has been a long-standing debate over economic *versus* non-economic causes. Particularly among those approaching migration in terms of individual motivations, there has been a concern to avoid simplistic economic reductionism. David Parkin, for example, has argued that migration patterns typically differ between ethnic groups in Africa, or take place in the context of ethnic competition; since such ethnic groups are *defined*, in his terms, by socio-cultural and ideological factors, these must be included in the analysis.[6] But, pushed to its extreme, the attempt to separate non-economic from economic factors can lead to analyses verging on the absurd. As Samir Amin put it, the Zarma may go to Kumasi as they used to go to war in the past, but they do not do so because they have an 'adventurous temperament'. They do so because the capitalist system obliges them to earn money:

Just as the same colonial system forbade them to wage war, migration inevitably replaced military adventure in their ideology. A necessity became an ideal. Questioned as to the reasons for their migration, certain Zarma replied that they go to earn money to pay the taxes, and others for adventure. The survey of motivations, by which some sociologists believe they can separate economic from extra-economic motivations, is in reality useless because the economic reason is there in every case and its ideological guise is equally general.[7]

In this book we take the view that the various 'ethnic'

patterns referred to by Parkin should be seen instead as systems of social production relations, which are interwoven complexes of 'economic' and 'ideological' factors, but whose underlying dynamic is in a broad sense economic. Individual motivations will reflect this combination of ideological and economic factors.

Analysis must take place both on the level of the political economy of each of the two modes of production the worker is involved in, as peasant and as wage laborer, and on the level of individual experience and action in each arena. It is insufficient to construct a theory of the quantities, directions or causes of migration flows on the basis of individual or even household decision-making, to the neglect of the political–economic structures, as many neoclassical economists do.[8] In this approach the assumption of individual or group utility maximization, whether utility is seen solely in terms of material income or in terms of more diffuse social values, implies a degree of voluntarism on the part of individuals that is quite far removed from African social and economic reality. In addition, these works tend to focus on the decision to migrate, not on the decision to return home, even if the latter might also be 'explained' in terms of neoclassical assumptions. Finally, when these analyses focus on households as utility maximizers, they usually fail to disaggregate the differing positions of material and political power *within* households and families, leading to a neglect of the constraints under which women and children, in particular, operate. This is not to say, however, that analysis at the individual and household levels should be abandoned, but rather that it should be organically linked to its larger context. In Chapters 1 and 2 we focus on the broader political–economic processes, but in Chapter 3 we move to the household level. In the remaining part of Chapter 1, we turn to the question of the internal and/or external origins of labor migrancy in Africa.

ORIGINS OF MIGRANT LABOR

One of the most fundamental controversies about migrant labor in Africa concerns its origins: did the pattern of part-time wage earning have its causes wholly in the logic of the externally imposed capitalist mode of production, in the capitalists' need for cheap labor, or were there any features of pre-capitalist society or ecology which contributed to this outcome? In this section we take the view that capitalism was not immediately omnipotent in the face of all local conditions, and that it was the interaction between capitalism and the various pre-existing African economies that determined that part-time migrant labor would be the predominant wage-earning pattern.

The argument for largely external causation developed out of an influential set of articles on South Africa by Harold Wolpe and Martin Legassick,[9] which explicated the economic logic of the migrant pattern from the capitalist perspective. Because of the subsidy provided by the worker's periodic return to the continuing subsistence economy, he could be paid a wage insufficient to provide all his basic, essential needs. A 'bachelor wage' supported a single male during his working days, while the rural economy supported his parents, wife, children, and the worker himself in his old age. Migrant labor therefore equalled cheap labor; no provision was made for workers' retirement or social security, and little investment in training or education was necessary since most labor was unskilled or semi-skilled. As a final plus for the capitalist, migrant labor is also sometimes thought to be docile labor, since strikes and labor organizing are difficult with high labor turnover.

The first consideration that suggests the need for modification of this line of argument is that, without the two elements of coercion and rural impoverishment which came to be associated with migrant labor in Africa, the system was not necessarily cheap. Where peasant or subsistence incomes were high, for example, Africans raised the supply price of their labor. In some cases in nineteenth-century southern Africa, the supply was controlled by still independent chiefs, who restricted the flow of labor in order to keep the price high. On the demand side, the number of new enterprises in most areas soon exhausted the easily available labor supply, and competition among employers kept wages up. Again the prime example is South Africa, where, until the monopsonistic organization of recruiting and wage determination came into full effect at the beginning of the twentieth century, migrant labor was in fact expensive in comparison to the wages prevailing in Europe at the time.[10] It took some time for capitalism and capitalist coercion to penetrate and undermine rural economies enough to establish the low-wage tradition.

Second, the coercive recruiting systems themselves were not inexpensive.[11] In areas like Katanga, Southern Rhodesia and South Africa, mining interests either administered their own systems or hired recruiting companies. Into the total social costs of the migrant system have to be figured the costs of enforced recruitment (capitation fees and travel expenses paid to recruiters); losses through desertion, high turnover, theft and lack of skill; and the costs of the controlled compound system. When one considers these total costs to employers or the state, it is not clear that coercive migrant labor was really any cheaper than some other labor systems that have been common on the periphery of the world capitalist system. Slavery, share-cropping, labor tenancy, and debt-peonage have all served essentially the same purpose of coercing cheap semi-proletarianized labor in a context of limited capitalization. Yet migrancy was clearly the most widespread system used in Africa, slavery and labor tenancy being only minor themes.[12]

In the earliest years of industrial development in Africa, employers themselves were by no means certain what system of labor mobilization would work best. Shula Marks has pointed to the fact that some mining industrialists in South Africa would have preferred to see a more fully proletarianized labor force, while others leaned towards a bondage system akin to slavery.[13] The argument over stabilization *versus* migrancy raged among Rhodesian mineowners as well;[14] and, in agriculture in Kenya and elsewhere, white settlers initially adopted tenant farming, squatter, or in Portuguese territories even slave, systems before going over to exclusive reliance on migrants. It appears, then, that migrancy was not the *only* system which could satisfy the capitalist demand for cheap, tractable labor. Whether it was the optimum system depended to a great degree on the technical organization of production, particularly the level of capitalization, which varied a great deal from industry to industry and colony to colony, as Charles Perrings has pointed out.[15] Nonetheless, for a full explanation of the emergence of migrant labor in Africa, we must look not only at the capitalists' demands for labor but also at certain aspects of the supply situation.

The access of the great majority of Africans to land adequate for subsistence militated against full proletarianization throughout most of the colonial period. The relatively low man:land ratio in this part of the Third World, combined with the crucial importance of human labor inputs in most of the low-technology horticultural systems, made labor a scarce and valued resource in traditional agriculture. These factors, together with the lack of any large landless class in African societies, posed a strong intrinsic barrier to the development of full-time wage labor. At the same time, in the absence of coercion or underdevelopment, these conditions made early migrant labor expensive, inefficient and inadequate in supply.

Before coercive measures were imposed, almost all mineowners, settlers and railway builders were plagued by severe labor shortages.

On the other hand, there were at least three characteristics widely found in pre-colonial African societies which enhanced the likelihood that at least some groups of Africans would respond positively to the opportunity of parttime, migrant labor without any coercion being necessary. First, the generally low level of technology used in African agriculture meant that some societies suffered from unpredictability of food supplies. Ecological and climatic factors, such as drought, tsetse fly, locusts or rinderpest epidemics, could disrupt food supplies or kill off livestock. Groups raided by more powerful neighbors, or farming on marginal lands, were especially vulnerable. Drought (known as *shangwa*), for example, periodically disrupted fragile Shona agriculture and played an important role in encouraging Shona to take up wage work in the Kimberley diamond mines in the 1870s and the Rhodesian gold mines in the 1890s.[16] Drought, too, drove the Kamba in Kenya to turn up for railway work in 1899 for the first time.[17] The rinderpest epidemic, which destroyed the majority of African cattle in southern Africa in 1896–9, contributed greatly to the proletarianization of Africans, since those who lacked cash had to make more migratory journeys in order to restock. The railway between Bechuanaland and Rhodesia was built largely with such 'rinderpest labor'.[18]

Second, the divisions of labor and of social roles that were broadly characteristic of most African societies determined that, if any group was to be available for wage labor, it would be the 'young men', although in some West African societies it was, in the first instance, the household slaves. As described more fully in Chapter 3, the main social divisions lay between the politically powerful elders and the junior males on the one hand, and between men and women

Migration and development

on the other. In the actual labor of subsistence, there was everywhere an important distinction between men's and women's roles. Except in those few societies that had adopted the plough, the bulk of the planting, cultivating, harvesting and processing of crops was done by women.[19] The men's role in agriculture was mainly to clear the land; housebuilding, warfare, raiding, hunting, cattle-keeping and long-distance trade were men's other subsistence contributions. These roles, however, were precisely those that were more vulnerable to disruption by commercial capitalism and European conquest. Warfare and raiding were gradually stamped out by colonial administrations, 'structural unemployment' thereby being introduced in some societies. One form of raiding which yielded a commodity for the capitalist market – slave raiding – gradually died out under the impact of the British worldwide anti-slavery campaign, again depriving some groups of a source of income. Raiding the wild animals for marketable commodities – hides, skins, ivory – soon reached ecological limits in many areas. Elephant and other game populations were seriously depleted. Other forms of long-distance trade, in cattle or foodstuffs, were also subject to the vicissitudes of the market; trade might flourish for a while, as European development created new demands for food supplies, or it might decline quickly under the impact of restrictive regulations or competition from European farmers. As the cases below illustrate, some African societies grew and prospered on the basis of such long-distance trade, only to find themselves under stress when the markets died out or were taken over by others.

Such situations disrupted men's roles more than women's, and as opportunities for short-term wage labor opened up, men shifted into them, leaving the women to carry on subsistence production. In this way, African stereotypes as to the proper division of labor between men and women combined with European ones to ensure that it was men who initially took up wage earning.

The changes in men's roles shed light on the seeming adaptability of some African societies to periodic, long-distance labor migration. Some features of migrant labor were similar to men's traditional social roles. In those societies which had depended on long-distance trade, men were already familiar with lengthy traveling, and, although the routes to the mines and the farms were usually different, once they were learned men would arrive there in groups, as they would for trade. In other cases, we know that the men enjoyed the link between the old and the new roles; among the Kenya Luo, for example, they referred to wage work as 'raiding' the white man's economy.[20] Among the Ovambo in Angola, as raiding and trading were increasingly curtailed by the colonial system, 'it would appear that there occurred a form of culture transfer in favour of migrant labour'.[21] But ultimately Africans were even less able to control the terms of exchange in the labor market than they had been in their long-distance trade or raiding activities.[22]

If the security of the material base and the social organization of productive labor varied a great deal from society to society in Africa, so also did the final important factor which affected the response of African societies to wage labor in the absence of coercion: the strength of patriarchal control by elders. What is important here is not political centralization, but rather the extent to which elders, chiefs or kings controlled the labor time of junior males or other dependent clans or ethnic groups, either within or outside households. In the more highly stratified societies an effective decision might be made by the king or chiefs to send out the young men to wage labor – or alternatively to resist wage earning. Such a decision would reflect the rulers' assessment of the whole material and military situation, *vis-à-vis* neighbors or encroaching white

Migration and development

settlers. The Pedi, discussed below, offer a striking example of the rulers' attempt to manipulate the wage-labor system, in this case for the purpose of getting firearms for territorial defense.

Pierre-Philippe Rey has pointed out that collaboration of the pre-capitalist rulers with capitalists in the supply of labor has historically been an important factor in the transition to capitalism.[23] Such was the case in Africa as well. But it is not correct to say, as Rey does, that hierarchical or centralized societies were necessarily willing to produce forced labor for the capitalists, or that they were the only ones from which migrant labor came. The control of the elders over the actions of the 'young men' could be strong even in highly segmentary societies, as Chapter 3 points out; even where such control was weak, widespread labor migration could still emerge.

Where elders had less control, labor migration, to a greater extent than some earlier forms of economic endeavor, could be a 'strategy employed by "cadets" in an attempt to outflank the control of the elders over bridewealth'.[24] The potential for economic independence for individual young men or their separate households arose out of the individualism implicit in capitalism; the employer generally paid the wage to the worker himself and not to his chief or family, although, as we shall see, deferred payment to the chiefs later became a method of control over migrant workers. The potential for wage work to lead to individual independence was not lost on the elders and chiefs, however; they usually attempted to blunt the threat in some way – through tribute, tax or insistence on periodic return – though with varying degrees of success. Significantly, in the early cases of 'voluntary' participation in wage labor, it was more often the traditional rulers than the capitalists who were vitally concerned that the contract be short-term rather than long-term, and that the migration be not permanent.[25] Thus labor migration introduced a struggle not only between the African and European ruling groups, but also between the elders and junior males within African societies, between the beneficiaries of the traditional system and those who initially saw in wage labor an opportunity to better their situation. This dynamic, as well as the others noted above, can be seen in the cases of the Tsonga, the Pedi and the Ovambo, all of whom began participating in wage labor before the onset of widespread labor coercion.

The experience of the Tsonga, in southern Mozambique, illustrates how both internal and external factors, operating at different periods, must be combined to explain participation in wage labor. Tsonga began migrating to the labor markets of the Cape and Natal in the 1850s; by the 1890s at least half of the able-bodied men were going out to work, and of these some 30–40% did not return. In the 1850s and 1860s there was a large permanent migration of Tsonga, both families and single workers, into South Africa. Many of them settled under Shangaan or Nguni chiefs in Natal; in migrating from there to South African and Rhodesian mines they became known as 'Shangaans', and were among the most skilled and highly paid underground workers.[26] All of this took place before the imposition of Portuguese rule in 1895–7, since before this time Portuguese control did not extend beyond the trading depot of Lourenço Marques (now Maputo).

Why did the Tsonga and Chopi groups in this area move so quickly and in such numbers into migrant labor? The economic causes probably lie in a combination of tribal warfare, loss of trade monopolies, decline of cattle-herding and agriculture due to ecological setbacks, decline of local game-hunting, and capitalist competition. The Nguni incursions beginning in the 1820s disrupted the previously profitable external trade in ivory and rhinoceros horn; they established a monopoly in the ivory trade, eliminating

Tsonga profits. The importation of cattle into the area from the west, important to the local economy, was also disrupted both by Nguni expansion and by British and Afrikaaner penetration. The Nguni also raided Tsonga and Chopi for cattle and slaves, and impressed some men into their armies. In addition to the effects of the Nguni, the external trade itself was being limited by the decline of elephant and other game in the area. The difficulties in getting cattle, formerly the chief currency of *lobolo* (or bridewealth), affected the marriage system. In addition, a general poverty was engendered by – or engendered – a series of epidemics of smallpox, typhoid, and blackwater fever. While the full extent and interrelation of these changes are not yet fully understood, it seems clear that their cumulative impact was to predispose many Tsonga to migrate in search of better options.[27]

It is significant that in a period before the South African state had imposed contracted recruiting, pass laws, prosecution of deserters and other laws aimed at controlling labor to insure its return home after short-term employment, workers from southern Mozambique returned home 'voluntarily'. Seasonal demands of agriculture are surely one reason; but, even more important, chiefs and elders attempted to retain control over migrant laborers. By limiting the time they spent at work, they could mitigate the disruptive effects on rural society.[28]

Control of marriage was central, since this was the point at which a young man established his independence from his paternal household. Marriage required bridewealth, and it was the young man's potentially independent access to it *via* wages that threatened paternal control. Whereas before the 1860s bridewealth had been paid in cattle, drought and epidemic had forced a switch to iron hoes, a currency which was likewise controlled by the *numzane*, or elders, since they were the only ones with resources enough to afford them. But increasingly young men who earned wages in South Africa could afford hoes, buying them with sterling specie. By the mid-1870s sterling was rapidly replacing hoes as the medium of bridewealth. The *numzane* could not prevent this conversion; instead, they continually raised the bride price, fairly successfully keeping it above the level of the returning migrant's resources.

Second, the elders imposed heavy taxation on workers. The amount of direct tax on wages varied from chiefdom to chiefdom, but in addition there were various other fines and prestations. Among the Mabudu, for example, the chief used labor regiments to plant and weed his fields, and all those young men who avoided the work by going to South Africa were fined £5–10. Chiefs also made money by charging outside labor recruiters for the right to operate and for the number of subjects recruited. A final way in which elders retained control was by lowering the marriage age for girls and boys from the mid-twenties to eleven or thirteen years. This pushed young men into marriage *before* migrating, thus continuing their dependence on elders for bride price and ensuring that the pull of family ties would draw the young men home again.

The way in which male labor migration was facilitated by shifting more of the homestead work on to women is also illustrated in the Tsonga case. The reduction in marriage age meant that women became mothers much younger. By the 1890s women performed felling and burning of trees, once male tasks, as well as field-watching and harvesting.[29] In other areas of southern Africa the adoption of the plough intensified the male role in agriculture, but this effect was not evident in Tsongaland, where the plough was unsuitable for the sandy soils.[30]

Although the Tsonga elders were active in trying to retain control of migration, they did not form a highly centralized society. This example therefore refutes Rey's hypothesis that only highly centralized societies responded in a positive way to labor migration. Here the impetus to migrate came from the young men, the elders having to work hard to retain control. The Pedi, another group to appear early in the South African labor market, were somewhat more centralized, and their chiefs played a greater role in instigating migration.

A similar constellation of economic factors predisposed the Pedi to labor migration: reduction of trade networks, limited agricultural success (due in this case to low and erratic rainfall) and, in the early years, the disruptive effects of the *difaqane*, the wars in the wake of the rise of the Zulu kingdom in the first decade of the twentieth century.[31]

By the 1860s the Pedi were migrating in large numbers from the north-eastern Transvaal to the Cape Colony each year. With the money they earned they bought guns and ammunition before returning home. Men traveled in groups as large as 200. It took two weeks to reach their first stopping-point, the Basotho kingdom ruled by Mshweshwe, from where, after performing service or paying tribute to get an exit permit, they moved on to the Cape Colony. There they worked for at least as long as it took to purchase a gun, but sometimes for up to two years. Returning migrants waited in Mshweshwe's area until a large group had assembled, then made the hazardous trip north, risking attack both from Afrikaaners, anxious to prevent Africans from getting guns, and from other groups of Africans anxious to get them.

The opening of the diamond-mines in the early 1870s created a rapidly expanding market for African labor, and the Pedi responded with rapidity and on a large scale. Pedi and Tsonga were major sources of labor for these fields. Since wages were comparatively high for southern Africa, they could spend only four to eight months away from home and still afford a gun.

The attempts by Pedi chiefs and elders to manage labor migration are similar to those of the Tsonga, but what is different is the apparent single-mindedness with which wage labor was pursued as a strategy for building up the military position of the Pedi. Beginning in the early 1850s, the Pedi were under severe threat from the Zulu, the Swazi and the Afrikaans Trekkers. That they survived numerous attacks in this period testifies to the critical importance of firearms to them. In addition, guns were important in hunting, which in the 1860s provided a key supplement to cattle-keeping. It provided not only meat but also trade goods: skins, horns, ivory and feathers. Later, however, the eradication of game led to its decline.

Having become dependent on this imported and changing technology, the Pedi had to continue migrating in order to keep up with gun technology and retain their military advantage. Other southern African societies were also getting access to firearms; what is unusual about the Pedi is that they did it so early and through labor migration only. In the context of regional economic and military competition, the Pedi specialized in migrant labor – because they had no flourishing markets in which to trade cattle or grain for guns, as did some other groups.

Pedi chiefs could not, however, retain control over the guns themselves. In fact, general distribution of them was probably in the interest of all. Chiefs did, however, accumulate stores of ammunition to be distributed among the populace in times of war. Chiefs also exacted tribute in the form of gifts from the returning laborers – and had various sub-chiefs and deputies on the diamond-fields and other work-sites to keep tabs on them. But an attempt to exact a fixed amount of tribute at the work-site prior to the worker's acquisition of a gun apparently failed.

The Sotho kingdom in the late nineteenth century is an even more striking example of the way in which chiefs organized labor migration with the intention of ensuring an armed populace. But here the migration was even less 'voluntary' – not only because it was organized by the chiefs and because the ruling Koena lineage extracted much labor service and other forms of surplus, but also because formal independence had been brought to an end in 1868 and, although a fierce Gun War was fought (and won) against the Cape Colony government from 1881 to 1884, some colonial administrative pressures, and a hut tax, operated in addition to chiefly pressures toward wage labor. By the 1870s the new phenomenon of impoverished and landless households forced to migrate to fulfill basic needs, especially in order to meet the tax in cash, had emerged.[32]

It is relevant to the Tsonga, the Pedi and the Sotho cases that in the early years of development of gold- and diamond-mines in South Africa, and the greatly expanded demand for labor, competition for it between employers made it necessary to offer high wages – and to allow the easy availability of guns. Not surprisingly, government officials were unhappy with the situation and attempted to stop the gun trade, making it in many areas illegal. The trade nonetheless flourished, while large employers looked the other way. If guns were what it took to attract Africans into the labor market, they were prepared to take the risk.

Labor migration as the last resort after the enforced decline of ivory, slave and cattle trading, consequent upon the gradual extension of Portuguese military control, is the keynote of the Ovambo experience in Angola.[33] As in other areas, initial contact with European capitalist markets stimulated a growth in trade, on which were built powerful kingships and royal clans. From the mid-1840s trade was mainly to meet the European demand for ivory, and there were few formal attempts to colonize the area. From then until about 1900 cattle replaced ivory as the mainstay of trade; in all these and earlier years slaves had also been exported. Cattle were sold to the Portuguese at the coast or to the South Africans, and slaves were either ransomed, sold to the Portuguese, or incorporated into the productive systems of the Ovambo, allowing them to increase the size of the fields under cultivation.

The Ovambo obtained all of these items by raiding neighboring groups, and in this the acquisition of firearms from the Europeans greatly enhanced their productivity. These were also important in hunting; but surrounding groups were also beginning to acquire arms, and therefore continued needs for firearms became a necessity for preserving societal independence as well as economic advantage. The trade to acquire firearms directly enhanced the productive base and the security of Ovambo society, and for them was not simply a matter of luxuries or consumption goods.

Unfortunately the initial burst of trading proved unsustainable. Within three decades the elephants were all but destroyed, leading to increasing emphasis on cattle and slave raiding. By the 1890s the Ovambo were hard put to it to keep increasing their numbers of cattle, and some kings were over-taxing their subjects, leading to a large build-up of cattle in kings' courts at the expense of commoners. The climax came in the form of a natural disaster, the rinderpest epidemic, which reached Ovamboland in 1897 and killed off 90% of the cattle. Between the 1880s and 1900 the Portuguese and Germans gradually gained control of the surrounding areas. The drying-up of South African markets, together with Portuguese intervention, contributed to the end of cattle trading. Rinderpest was followed by a long series of drought years, interspersed with floods and plagues of locusts, culminating in the terrible famines of 1911 and 1915. The Ovambo attempted to recoup through more raiding, but they found their neighbors as badly hit as they were. Raiding was also increasingly stopped by the

Portuguese, who were gearing up to conquer the area. Setting up a chain of forts, they attempted to ban Ovambo trade altogether, to prevent Africans from getting arms. Final Portuguese military conquest came in 1915–17.

The Ovambo kings were unable to recover from these blows. Whereas they had once made great profits from trade, they now fell into ever-increasing debt to traders. They imposed internal taxation, and the traditional seizure of cattle was now imposed in a harsh and arbitrary way by a specialized army of tax-collectors. A new social stratum, of households without cattle, emerged, and although the production by women of the agricultural staple, millet, continued, it *was* hit by the drought, flood and locusts.

The major response to this pauperization was the development of migrant labor. These internal changes in Ovambo coincided with the sudden expansion in colonial demand for labor. In Angola this was due to the construction of the Mossamedes and Benguela railways from 1904, and to plantations and fisheries at the coast, especially after the formal abolition of slavery in 1911. Much labor went to Namibia for work in German plantations, copper- and diamond-mines and railways. Some areas of Ovambo were conquered by the Portuguese by 1907, and a hut tax was introduced, creating an additional pressure on labor. By 1914 about 10,000 men per annum went out from Ovamboland for labor. However, the survival of crop cultivation, and the traditional and colonial authorities, combined to limit proletarianization to recurrent migrancy.

In this case, as among the Sotho to a lesser extent, the growth of an internal impoverished stratum was another key factor in labor migration. And although the kings here do not appear to have actively organized migration, they did attempt to profit from it and to limit its disruptive effects on rural society. Workers were allowed to leave for periods of only six months, and only at times which harmonized with the agricultural cycle. Workers traveled in groups under a leader and were able to demand that they be hired as a group, 'maintaining cohesion and discipline on lines reminiscent of the raiding parties'.[34] Royal control could not, however, prevent the formation of Ovambo settlements in towns and at missions.

In some cases wage labor emerged not out of the sort of competition and catastrophic reversals suffered by the Tsonga, Pedi and Ovambo, but in a more evolutionary fashion. One form this took can be seen in the early Nigerian tin-mines, where Africans who had worked alluvial and shallow-pit gold or tin deposits as independent prospectors and traders were then taken on as employees by the European companies to whom the colonial state had granted prospecting licenses or mining leases. We do not know whether the change was seen as a loss or a gain by the workers, but formally at least it is akin to the subjection of independent artisans to capital in Western European history. Another traditional arrangement which glided easily into wage labor was seasonal migrations during the dry season in West Africa to place one's self and one's family in the service of those who were better off. In the Nigerian tin-mines one source of early voluntary labor was found in this Hausa custom of *cin rani* (literally 'eating the dry season', or eating other people's food during the dry season). Since compounds were not employed at these mines, and families were allowed to live nearby, work at the mines simply took the place of other less commercialized forms of work that these migrants might have found. In this case, wage work solved a perennial subsistence problem.[35]

A third kind of transformation of a pre-capitalist institution into wage labor can be seen in the practice of hiring Africans who were, or had been, household slaves. This could take place in evolutionary fashion, as when European caravans exploring the interior of East Africa hired porters who were nominally slaves of Arab overlords in the coastal towns. Often the slaves were required to give a portion of their wages to their masters when they returned. Similarly, Hausa slave-owners allowed their slaves to work in the Nigerian tin-mines during the dry season; a perhaps unforeseen result was that some of them were able to pay for their own manumission with the proceeds. A few years later, when the British abolished slavery in these areas, ex-slaves who could not get access to productive land were willing to work for wages.[36] The abolition of slavery often encountered African resistance, however, as among the Baule of the Ivory Coast.[37] The French settled ex-slaves in *villages de liberté* and then called on them for forced labor.

Slaves destined for export to the Americas also contributed to the African supply. In southern Angola Portuguese fishermen and plantation owners used slaves as their main labor supply from 1840 to 1878, since the suppression of the Atlantic slave trade in the 1840s had led to a glut of locally available slaves, while the indigenous population was small and unwilling to work for wages. Even though legally abolished in 1878, slavery under various guises continued to be widely used in Portuguese territories until 1911, when genuine abolition took place. After that most ex-slaves became wage workers. Slavery had in fact prepared the ground for wage labor, because the masters had been forced by the state to pay a token wage to their *serviçaes* after 1880, so that the wage form was in a sense already established.[38]

These instances illustrate why some African societies, or categories of people within those societies, turned to migrant labor without coercion by the state. But perhaps the most characteristic African response to the wage option, before state coercive pressures were applied, was to ignore or avoid it. A good many African societies were in the fortunate position of wanting very little from the capitalist economy and of being willing to trade only goods, not services, for those things. Many cattle-keeping groups, such as the Maasai in Kenya, were in this category. The only form of labor which the Maasai were willing to supply was military, and that was in the form of labor tribute, or labor service, to an ally, rather than in the form of wage labor. By the turn of the century, Maasai herds had been built up again after the natural disasters and military reverses of the previous decades. The rich supply of livestock made it possible for the Maasai to resist almost completely the strong pressures to join the labor market which were applied in this settler economy. They paid their taxes through the sale of cattle and animal products, and their reserve, though subsequently reduced in size despite their loyal allegiance, remained adequate.

Another point of contrast between the Maasai and the Tsonga, Pedi and Ovambo was the relative independence and coherence of the *moran* or warrior age-group. Unlike other societies, the Maasai elders and ritual leaders were unable to enforce on the *moran* the decline in status that non-military wage earning appeared to entail. Settlers who, like Lord Delamere, managed to employ Maasai as herdsmen found them 'haughty' and 'arrogant'.[39] In the Maasai case we see the main factors which tended to make it possible for African societies to decline labor migration: relative security of material base, continuance of viable alternative economic roles for junior males, lack of an exploited or under-privileged social category whom whites would hire,[40] and lack of any effective initiatives in the direction of wage labor by the leaders or chiefs.

LABOR COERCION

Important as the early 'free-market' supply of labor was, it was almost everywhere inadequate to meet the demands of European administrative, mining, railway and farming enterprises. Despite the aspects of their material situation and social structure that predisposed some African societies toward part-time wage labor, the more significant fact is that the lineage mode of production, in most of its variants and under most conditions, did not yield a very large supply of wage labor even where a large demand for it was created.

The difficulties faced by early settlers and other employers in securing wage labor are well known. The supply was inadequate, of course, at the prices the employers were willing to pay; had they been in a position to raise wages, more workers might have been forthcoming. Employers varied in their financial capabilities, from Afrikaans settlers and Indian store-owners operating on a shoestring, to transnational mining conglomerates and state-backed enterprises. But in the end nearly every colonial government rescued employers by enacting a battery of labor-coercive measures.

Comparatively, direct coercion and state-engineered rural underdevelopment played a far greater role in the creation of an African labor force than they did in European or American labor history, or in many other parts of the Third World. What the enclosures and population growth accomplished in England, and over population and rural stratification in Asia, state coercion and manipulation did in Africa. However, South Africa is the only African society to have industrialized on the basis of a mainly coerced labor supply, and indeed its 'labor repressive' industrialization policies have important similarities to those of such states as Prussia and the Soviet Union.

The chief mechanisms in the creation of a semi-proletariat may be simply listed. First, the conquest and active administration of African societies was usually accompanied by a) taxation; b) exhortations from district administrators about the moral value of wage employment for men, and incentives and pressures on government-appointed chiefs to send out laborers; and c) direct forced labor. Second, employers themselves, sanctioned by colonial states, often became heavily involved both in coercive recruiting on the one side and, on the other, in coercion at the sites of production through closed compounds. Third, there were more indirect measures involving land. A series of enactments in settler and mining areas deprived Africans of land and often confined growing populations to limited 'reserves'. Land was given over to white settlers and mining companies. In areas of white agriculture, a host of government subsidies was given to white farmers and denied to black ones, subsidies ranging from preferential rail-rates and new rail-lines to government technical assistance, favorable loans, discriminatory quality control regulations, and crop restrictions for Africans. Herein lie the roots of the underdevelopment of African agriculture which was so potent a cause of labor out-migration by the 1920s. Finally, labor control was further supported by the state through the enforcement of criminal sanctions against 'breach of contract' – that is, strikes or desertions. In South Africa the control of labor also involved the pass laws and the institutionalization of migrancy through the denial to Africans of any permanent citizenship in the urban or industrial areas.

Colonial strategies to force the African to work, and African reactions to them, are discussed in Chapter 4. Here we comment briefly on the impact of taxation. Taxation as a method of forcing out laborers did raise the cash cost of living for Africans, but it did not distinguish between various sources of cash. Most Africans who could simply sold produce or livestock in order to pay the tax. But where Africans were poor in items to sell, or were distant from markets, taxation could produce laborers. Contrasting responses to the imposition of taxation can be illustrated in the case of northern Nyasaland (Malawi).

'Nyasas' from the Ngoni-dominated northern part of the territory were prominent in the early supply of labor to Rhodesian and Transvaal mines, and part of the explanation lies in conditions similar to those affecting the Ovambo: the colonial disruption of Ngoni regional dominance, slave-trading and stock-raiding. Some of the agricultural peoples whom the Ngoni exploited experienced something of a renaissance, but the Ngoni themselves were forced to turn to labor migration.[41] An additional important factor here was the imposition of a Sh. 3 annual hut tax over the whole colony in 1896. This was a high figure for the northern areas who were far from the main European agricultural settlements in the south, and undoubtedly stimulated further migration.

In the south of Malawi, however, Africans preferred to meet the tax by growing maize and vegetables for the local market and by brewing beer for workers. Southern planters, therefore, were short labor, and pressed for an even higher tax. As a result the tax was raised in 1901 to Shs. 6, with a Sh. 3 remission for those who could prove they had worked for a European for at least one month. This 'labor tax' had an immediate effect. The labor market in the south became flooded, and those who were unwilling to migrate abroad had to return home empty-handed. When the tax began to be collected, hundreds of men in areas close to Portuguese East Africa fled the country and built temporary grass huts across the border until the tax collectors had left.[42]

This case illustrates that taxation also did not discriminate as to employers within a regional economic system. Where low-wage agricultural employers competed with high-wage mining companies, the former lost out. This was the case in southern Rhodesia, where local mine employers competed with the Transvaal mines for labor, and the imposition of a massive tax increase such as that in 1904 mainly benefited the Transvaal.[43]

Taxation, then, if it were high enough and applied under other conditions of economic constraint, could force men into wage earning. However, it certainly cannot be the whole of the cause, since in most areas (Nyasaland, Kenya) the unskilled wage rates were such that one month's work was sufficient to pay the tax. There were many Africans who therefore worked only for one month, or perhaps for two or three to pay for costs of transport, for taxes of brothers, fathers and other kin or for some valued commodities. But it is also true that most migrants worked for far longer than a few months; indeed in most areas it was almost impossible not to, given the nature of the contract system. We must therefore look beyond taxation to ascertain the full force of the state pressures on Africans to join in migrant labor.

§ 2 §

MIGRANTS AND THE RURAL ECONOMY

Voluntary migration arose from the interaction of two factors: the introduced capitalist demand for labor, and certain inadequacies in some rural economies, though not their total collapse. As the colonial economy developed, force and other indirect non-market pressures vastly increased the numbers who participated, voluntarily or involuntarily, in migrant labor.

What is the cumulative effect on the rural economy of the prolonged large-scale involvement of men in migrancy? Is temporary migration capable of contributing to rural development, providing a new inflow of cash for investment in agricultural and commercial enterprises, as proponents of migration have claimed? Or is it at best a means of staving off rural starvation, and at worst, a pattern which invariably undercuts rural progress, in a self-reinforcing spiral of rural decline? Or are different outcomes possible in different places? And, to put the question in individual terms, can the migrant ever become an accumulator, a new bourgeois, or does he remain forever trapped in the pattern of oscillating migrancy? This chapter will be devoted to these questions.

The effect of migrancy on 'tribal life' has probably been the most studied of all questions about African labor. There is a rich tradition of scholarly concern, which dates back to the 1940s and the urban anthropologists of the Rhodes–

Livingstone Institute in Zambia. The first directors of the Institute, Godfrey Wilson and his wife Monica, were emphatic in their denunciation of both the economic and the social effects of circulatory migration. In his pioneering *Essay on the Economics of Detribalization in Northern Rhodesia* (1941–2),[1] Wilson was the first to argue for the systematic interrelations between migration, demographic imbalances in town and country, destruction of family life and impoverishment of rural areas. Other studies elaborated aspects of this view, among them Isaac Schapera's *Migrant Labour and Tribal Life* (1947),[2] focussing on negative cultural effects in Botswana, and P. H. Gulliver's *Labour Migration in a Rural Economy* (1955),[3] arguing against the 'pull' of 'bright lights' as a cause of migration in Tanzania, and pointing instead to rural decay. Godfrey Wilson's essay actually took up themes that had already been put forward by Audrey Richards in her pioneering work on the Bemba, *Land, Labour and Diet in Northern Rhodesia* (1939).[4] Carried out from 1932 to 1934, her study stressed the general impoverishment of the Bemba, their poor nutrition, listlessness and desultory social life, all due to the absence of some 50% of the able-bodied men, though the exact proportion away varied a good deal from village to village. Despite the fact that young male Bemba were predominant among workers in the mines of the Copperbelt, those at home suffered a hungry season of about two months every year before their millet crop ripened; they 'bought clothes with hunger' as Wilson put it. This view of deteriorating tribal life was corroborated by Margaret Read's study of the Ngoni in Zambia and Malawi,[5] by the Keiskammahoek Rural Survey and other researches by Monica Wilson in South Africa,[6] and, at least in its economic aspects, by Max Gluckman's work on the Barotse of Zambia.[7]

Yet in the 1950s researchers increasingly challenged this

view, discovering that migration in fact contributed to the 'cohesion' of African tribal life and to the perpetuation of certain forms of 'traditional' cultural values and practices. William Watson's *Tribal Cohesion in a Money Economy* (1958)[8] argued for the Mambwe of Zambia that they were in fact benefiting from labor migration and that the absence of 50% of the men did not hurt the subsistence economy. Migrants actively maintained ties to, and invested in, rural economic and social relations, reinforcing the values placed on agricultural endeavor and the extended family. Van Velson[9] argued much the same thing for the Tonga on the shores of Lake Nyasa in Malawi (who had 60–75% of adult men away for long periods of time), as did Elkan for Uganda.[10] This new view was too often overstated, however, and neglected those cases where many customs had indeed changed, and it too easily became a justification for low wages and lack of stabilization of African workers at their places of work. In addition all these studies were unduly synchronic, were snapshots at a single point in time. Perhaps a more historical approach might yield a fuller picture?

A recent generation of critical historians of eastern, central and southern Africa has resurrected the hypothesis of rural decline, in the context of the general theory of underdevelopment. It is one of the sad ironies of African history that European mining and land-grabbing in settler areas set in motion a brief 'era of peasant prosperity' for many Africans, which was then snuffed out by forced migrant labor. Early settlement and mineral prospecting opened up new markets for African-grown produce. Since most Africans at first continued to farm their own land or that of absentee white owners, or farmed as rent-paying squatters or share-croppers, many benefited from the increased sales of produce. The years 1870–1913 in South Africa,[11] 1890–1908 in Southern Rhodesia (Zimbabwe),[12] and 1901–26 in Kenya[13] saw an actual increase in the prosperity of Africans. In fact in nearly all of eastern, central and southern Africa, Africans were 'anxious and able to respond to early colonial market opportunity and ... for decades they could out-produce and out-perform European farming'.[14] But in the end the increased demand for mine and farm labor, together with state action in favor of white farming and against African agriculture, led to the decline of African production. From that point, the 'structural underdevelopment of the peasantry' became 'the other side of the coin of capitalist development'.[15] The decline, of course, was not due to labor migration alone, but to the whole complex of forces unleashed by capitalist development; nevertheless the theme of a direct inverse correlation between labor migration and decline of agricultural production has been implicit in these writings.

However, not all peasantries in these areas declined to the same degree, or in exact proportion to the amount of labor that they supplied. Closer analysis of the complex and variable process of proletarianization is necessary. Moreover, there was a limit to the process; in all areas it stopped short of full proletarianization. The smooth functioning of a migrant labor system required an economy of origin that could at least provide basic subsistence to women, children and the elderly, since wages were held to the 'bachelor minimum'. The ideal solution was one in which agricultural production remained sufficiently virile to provide for subsistence and absorb return migrants, but not so viable as to threaten the supply of cheap labor. Such a delicate balance was nearly impossible to achieve, and this, as Robin Cohen points out, was one of the central contradictions of the colonial political economy.[16] What happens when the balance cannot be maintained can be seen in contemporary South Africa, where, despite white assertions to the contrary, the rural areas can no longer adequately support their populations, and where illegal influx into the urban areas and urban unrest have to be contained with heavily repressive policies.

Even if it is broadly true that the dominant tendency of capitalist development with migrant labor has been to undermine, to retard, but at the same time to conserve, peasant and subsistence production, still there are many variations on the theme. Empirically we can categorize three general situations. First are areas where labor migration coexists with a functioning subsistence economy; not an economy of increasing food production or export crops, but functioning nevertheless. This is the classic migrant labor situation, illustrated below by the descriptions of the Mambwe and the Mossi in the 1950s. Then there are the areas in which labor migration coexists with extensive growing of cash crops and cannot, in most cases, be said to have undermined the rural economy. The Kikuyu of Kenya illustrate one variant of this situation, with lengthy, continuous and extensive involvement in wage labor; while the coffee- and cocoa-growing areas of Ghana, Nigeria and Cameroon illustrate other variants. Usually these are areas of net in-migration, since migrant labor is hired by African farmers, but sons of farmers and some of the poor in these areas have developed distinctive patterns of participation in wage labor, particularly at times of declining farm incomes. Finally, at the other extreme, are the areas where labor migration has become almost the sole sustainable source of income for the rural community, agricultural production having suffered a marked decline. Most black rural areas of South Africa today are in this 'labor reserve' category, and here might also be included the Bemba of the 1930s and present-day Upper Volta. Obviously the economic and social effects of migrancy have been different in each of these kinds of situations, and in fact it is already clear that even a three-part division is too limited a grid to accommodate the great variability of rural economies.

This chapter will argue that there is no simple inverse

relationship between the growth of labor exports and the decline of the peasant economy, that the trade-off between the two has not usually been a simple zero-sum game. For the African cases, there may well be some upper limit to the percentage of adult men away, or to the length of time they are away, above which one can say that agricultural production will necessarily in all cases decline. But below that limit the effect of male absence will vary according to such factors as population density, land availability, ecological constraints, type of crops, market prices for crops, farm technology, the social division of labor and socio-economic differentiation. This point was made with some force in the classic writings on migrancy of the 1950s,[17] but it deserves reemphasis for the new generation of academic researchers.

This chapter will deal only with the effects of migration on the economy and social relations of production, rather than discussing 'tribal cohesion' or the persistence of 'custom'. Some aspects of domestic relations are left to the next chapter. Limits of space dictate an exploration of only the main interconnections between the many variables involved. It is now fairly well established that a number of factors, including favorable ecology, new land, crop innovations, new technology and increased exploitation of women and children, can all compensate up to a point for the negative effects on agriculture of the withdrawal of male labor. On the other hand, another range of factors can nullify the possible positive effects of wage remittances; these include high bride prices, lack of productive investment opportunities, low produce prices and population increase under certain circumstances.

It has been suggested that the mere effect of the colonial imposition of an end to interethnic warfare and raiding accounts for the seemingly negative impact of migrant labor on the agriculture of some groups and its lack of such impact on others. Gluckman and others have pointed to a contrast in central Africa between the groups who lived largely by raiding their neighbors – such as the Bemba studied by Richards, the Ngoni studied by Read, and the Barotse studied by Gluckman – and those who were raided – the agriculturalists such as the Plateau Tonga and the Mambwe.[18] The former had a poorer agricultural base to begin with and when the *Pax Brittanica* was imposed suffered a relative loss, turning then to wage labor in great numbers. But low wages under the migrant system presumed a certain amount of supplementary family income from agriculture which these groups could no longer generate; hence their relative poverty, which struck Richards and other observers so forcefully. What seemed to be the result of high participation in wage labor was in fact traced to their poorly developed agriculture in the pre-colonial era.

The agriculturalists, on the other hand, benefited from the cessation of raids; as Watson points out for the Mambwe, they could reallocate the labor formerly used for defense into agriculture or wage labor, and they could keep all the crops they once lost. The Mambwe could move out of their former stockaded villages and live closer to their fields, could allocate cattle-herding to young boys instead of to men, who formerly had to protect herds from the Bemba, and could devote all time formerly spent on war, flight or guard duty to cultivation. Similar considerations apply to the Shona and Ndebele of Zimbabwe, the former of whom were raided by the latter.[19] A similar dynamic can be found in Kenya, although here the former raiders did not go into wage labor, except in a limited way as squatters and herders on European estates. The Kikuyu were raided by the Maasai, and the Luo were raided by the Nandi; in both cases the agriculturalists increased their production after colonial rule began, although the availability of new markets was also an important reason.

A second set of factors critical to the impact of migrant

labor lies in the nature of the agricultural and animal-husbandry systems, the first consideration being the centrality of the male role in the systems and the extent to which the labor of women and children was, or could be, substituted. There is considerable evidence from many societies that where subsistence production was kept up it was only because of an increased amount of labor by women – often, though not always, as a result of women taking on new tasks that formerly were done solely by men. Several examples are given below in Chapter 3. In the case of the Mambwe, as described by Watson in the 1950s, no changes in the culturally prescribed division of labor between men and women were necessary, only a probable increase in women's work-load. Watson reported that in the Mambwe grassland system of hoeing and green-manuring for the main subsistence crop of finger millet, the major work operations occurred only at concentrated periods and could be done by either men or women. Toward the end of a rainy season, the grassland was hoed up into wide piles inside which the grass decomposed quickly. At the beginning of the next rains, about January, they spread out the mounds and sowed millet. Some weeding was then required, done exclusively by women, and the crop was then harvested by the women in June, dried, thrashed and stored. Millet was rotated with beans or groundnuts, and after five to six years the field was fallowed. Hoeing was the only difficult part of this process, but both men and women did it, often in cooperative work parties.

This system contrasted with that of the neighboring Bemba, who inhabited a forest area in which the men lopped off the lower branches of trees, piled them on to the field, and burned them down to an ash seedbed for planting the millet. Here the presence of men to prune the trees was essential, and fields were simply not prepared if enough men were not present at the right time. However, some groups of forest Mambwe followed the same system as the Bemba – and yet still managed to produce enough food. This fact highlights two other aspects of Mambwe social organization which Watson considered crucial: the prevalence of cooperative work parties consisting of both men and women, and the presence in each village of core groups of men related to one another patrilineally.

The cooperative work party was the 'fundamental method of production' among the Mambwe.[20] The day before the work was to begin, the wife or wives of the household brewed beer. Large parties assembled and worked from about 8 o'clock in the morning until about 12 or 2 o'clock, hoeing, cutting trees, preparing seedbeds. When they returned from the fields, they all shared in the beer that had been prepared. The obligation to participate in such work groups was reciprocal; a person who participated in many work groups could expect that someone from each of the households involved would show up to cultivate his fields in return. In this way a wife whose husband was away at work in the mines could still be assured of having her garden prepared. This was the case even among the forest Mambwe, among whom, in contrast to the grassland groups in which there were no specialized roles for men, men were specifically needed to cut the tree branches once a year. There were still enough men available in each village in the 1950s, even with 50% away, to get all the trees cut.[21] Among the Bemba, by contrast, there was apparently little attempt at cooperative work.

Watson also argued that patrilineal societies such as the Mambwe were better able to withstand the absence of male labor than were matrilineal uxorilocal ones such as the Bemba.[22] Among the latter the man married into the matrilineage and moved to the village of his wife for a number of years to perform bride service for his father-in-law. He then often moved back to his own relatives' area to inherit land. The divorce rate was high. The man was therefore less likely to have a long-range interest in the agricultural prosperity of his wife's village; rather, if he invested in houses or equipment, this was more likely to be in the village of his own matrilineage. Watson suggested that the movement of men from village to village, in a system where their work role in agriculture was critical, was detrimental to production, by contrast to the more stable ties of the Mambwe men to one village. Mambwe village organization had a permanence that survived even the periodic changes of site required by slash-and-burn cultivation, and cemented the link between migrant males and their home. That matrilineality, as among the Bemba, could affect the propensity of newly married men to cooperate in work parties is a persuasive point, but it is less easy to see how it might affect men's general motivation to return home from wage work or to invest in rural areas. Even in matrilineal systems men do retain strong interests in their own matrilineage, though they may not actually inherit the land there until they are older, after working for some time as migrants. It is noteworthy that where residence practices were more variable within generally matrilineal societies, as among the Tonga studied by Van Velson, migrant labor did not seem to affect the male's role in agriculture.

Another aspect of the agriculture and husbandry systems that is obviously crucial is how much human labor input is required by the particular crops under cultivation, and with what frequency throughout the year. Cassava, for example, is a crop that gives a high output in weight and calories per invested labor-hour, by comparison to other widely planted traditional staples, such as millet in East Africa or yams in West Africa. In addition its cultivation can be done in small stints throughout the year, and when mature the tubers can be left in the ground for up to two years, depending on conditions, being harvested whenever the need or time occurs. Finally, it grows well even in unfertile land. The drawbacks are that the processing is time-consuming and the nutritional value is comparatively low. The fact that cassava formed the staple diet of the Tonga and that all its cultivation and harvesting was done by women, is a key reason why Van Velson could argue that labor migration did not at all disrupt rural production in that case.[23] Cotton-growing on the other hand, is very labor-intensive. The history of colonial government attempts to introduce its cultivation among groups heavily involved in migrant labor provides several case studies in official myopia. The British campaign in the 1930s to introduce cotton among the Kenya Luo and Luyia was a dismal failure, as was that of the French among the Mossi of Upper Volta.

The other side to this question is that of the labor demands of the wage economy; to what extent can migrant laborers synchronize their absences so that they can still contribute to agriculture at the time of peak labor demand? For many African societies the development of seasonal patterns of labor participation was the central factor in their adjustment to migrant labor. Watson reports that the Mambwe in the 1950s were able to approximate such a pattern, partly because they offered only unskilled labor to the mines. The older men in particular attempted to leave immediately after the main planting was finished for the year, in March and April, and to return after six to eight months in December or January, in time for the heavy cultivation at the beginning of the long rains. However, some 44% of the younger men were going away for from one to two years.[24]

Another group for whom seasonal labor has been a key to the preservation of food production are the Mossi of Upper Volta, as Elliott Skinner described them in the 1950s.[25] Like that of the Mambwe, their economy was still one of subsistence, and the amount of land available was sufficient though densely populated. But the Mossi inhabit a less ecologically advantageous area, food production came under more pressure, and the rate of more or less permanent out-migration was and is high.

In West Africa the coffee and cocoa areas of the Ivory Coast and Ghana have provided opportunities for wage labor to the societies of the inland, drier, savannah zone, such as the Mossi. Every year thousands of Mossi migrate south to the plantations, mines, transport networks and urban areas of the Coast. Mossi territory is relatively poor and infertile, but its pre-colonial economy was by no means poor. The area was densely populated, but subsistence activities included cultivation of millet, sorghum, maize and other crops, the herding of livestock, and long-distance trade in grains, livestock and locally produced cotton cloth. The social structure was complex; chiefs of large kingdoms ruled provinces, districts and villages headed by members of the royal lineage. There were nobles, commoners, serfs and slaves.[26]

With such a delicate balance of population and resources, it took only two factors to set long-distance migration in motion: the French imposition of a cash tax in 1896, at a time of some curtailment in their pre-colonial trade, and the imposition of forced labor for local work, from which long-distance absence could serve as an escape. Up to World War I taxes were raised gradually, forcing more and more Mossi to migrate. At this time migration was largely seasonal. In the 1920s the French intensified their exploitation of the area, and Mossi chiefs were made to recruit forcibly many thousands of workers. The *préstations* were forced day labor for the construction of roads, bridges and telegraph lines; there was also semi-forced contract labor for other administrative purposes and for private enterprises. Death-rates were rather high among such workers, and the pay was very low. Large numbers of Mossi were also forcibly conscripted into the French military, and there were several revolts against the excesses of military conscription during World War I. But the main form of resistance during these years was flight: individuals, indeed whole villages, would flee, often across the border to neighboring Ghana. Thus both labor emigration and local migrations were a form of resistance to taxes, forced labor, and forced crop collection.[27] After World War II forced labor was abolished in French colonies.

In 1955–7 some 80% of Mossi long-distance migrants were reported to follow a seasonal pattern. They did not leave until the crops had been harvested and the short but exacting period of agricultural work was over, at the end of November. After about five months working on coffee, cocoa and vegetable farms in Ghana or the Ivory Coast, they left that employment in April to return home for planting at the beginning of the rainy season. Most households started clearing the fields in April to be ready for the first rains in late May or early June, at which time millet, maize, sorghum and rice were sown. Those families whose migrants did not return at this time had to cut back on the sowing; if they did sow, the crops would become choked with weeds. Among these people, unlike the Mambwe, cooperative work parties, known as *sissosé*, used previously for clearing new fields, had declined. This work was done during the dry seasons and, with migrants away, most families were too busy compensating for absent men to participate.

Every year a certain percentage of Mossi migrants, about 20% in the 1950s, could not follow the seasonal pattern but instead worked on mines, roads and railroads for a number of years. Some were becoming more or less permanent town residents, but the existence of expatriate Mossi communities under the direction of chiefs facilitated the continuation of their customs, language and ties to their home territory.

Reports of agricultural officers in the 1950s were that food production had declined among the Mossi, owing to labor migration. Skinner could not directly verify this fact but did observe changes in the production system which suggested such a decline: for instance, the decrease in cultivation of small plots by individuals, both men and women, which were formerly used to supplement the staple grains grown on the household's collective plots, and over which each woman or man had personal control. Now, in most households nearly all labor had to be devoted to the group plot, the staple crop. Extras above and beyond subsistence, such as clothes and household goods, now depended on what the labor migrants could purchase. Migration thus to some extent made up for the decline in this part of subsistence cultivation.

Whatever the effect on subsistence, there was no development of cash-cropping here. Young men often compared their agriculture unfavorably to that of the cocoa areas where they worked, complaining that there was no profit in their own attempts. Another clearly adverse effect of migration was the decline in production of locally woven cloth, which formerly was both used and exported. There was a shortage of skilled weavers, since young men did not stay at home to learn to weave. Most cloth was imported from Europe, and cotton production itself was strongly undermined by the shortage of labor.

Today, Mossi migration continues, although the most frequent migrations are those to the Ivory Coast, the flow to Ghana having substantially decreased with the decline of the Ghanaian economy. Nowadays the greater part of the migration, perhaps one-half of all total out-migration, is for longer than just the agricultural season. Within Upper Volta, agricultural development remains limited. Between 1969 and 1973, there were some 200,000 out-migrations from the Mossi area, compared to only some 113,000 returns, indicating a rather large net loss in population. Migration is still, though, about four to one male.[28]

The Mossi and the Mambwe changed their cultivation system only in minor ways to compensate for the absence of males. Some groups, though, have made major adaptations, such as new crops and new technologies, which likewise stave off the adverse effects of the withdrawal of labor. One such case is that of the Mpondo in the South African Transkei, in the early years of their participation in the labor market.

In the three decades after 1910, the number of men migrating from Pondoland increased rapidly, from roughly 10,000 in 1910 to 30,000 in 1936. The percentage of the total population which was absent rose from about 9% to about 17%. Making certain assumptions, William Beinart estimates that about 25% of men between the ages of 15 and 45 were absent by 1910, and about 45% by 1936. Most households had a migrant, and these decades mark the period in which labor migrancy became a general experience throughout Mpondo society.[29]

At the same time, dramatic changes were taking place in agriculture. Sorghum cultivation was declining, being replaced by that of maize, which gave a higher although less consistent yield and which required less child labor. With the maize, mixed vegetables were sown. Cultivation could be done intensively, but at widely spaced intervals, since ox-drawn ploughs were being adopted. This new pattern fitted in well with labor migrancy and with the smaller peasant families brought about by the young men's new financial independence from their fathers' extended families. Between 1880 and 1920 the number of ploughs increased from 1,000 to an estimated 20,000; all homesteads must have owned or have had access to them by this time. Technology improved further with the introduction of steel ploughs and ox-drawn harrows in the 1920s. Purchases of these implements, and accumulation of an ox-team was often made possible by the wages from migrant labor.

The changes in cropping, which were integrally linked to migrancy, enabled all families to cultivate more land, despite their smaller size and the withdrawal of male labor for long periods. Male labor was now only essential in the ploughing, and perhaps in the harvest, seasons. From the late 1930s, if not earlier, the pattern of migration was assuming a marked seasonality. Migrants went to the goldmines, or to Johannesburg or to other towns. Where possible, they would leave home in December, January and February, taking a six- to nine-month contract and returning by October for ploughing.[30]

Total, and perhaps even *per capita*, output apparently continued to increase during the decades when mass migrancy became institutionalized. Statistics on crop production, while admittedly based on guesswork, suggest a fourfold if erratic increase in maize production between 1898 and 1939. Those on stockholding show a similar striking increase.[31] In interviews, many former migrants confirmed that they had been able to form the nucleus of a herd with their earnings at this time, partly because the cost of cattle was decreasing. Cattle provided milk, sheep provided wool, the goats could survive on pasturage where cattle could not, so at this time these were productive investments.

The agricultural changes did not allow the Mpondo household to become independent of wage income, but they did allow it at the very least to maintain production despite migrancy, and in most cases to increase it. However, after the 1930s crop production and stockholding almost certainly decreased, expansion having reached the limits of natural resources and of availability of capital, labor and markets. Thereafter, a spiral of declining production and rising impoverishment set in, until today the situation is similar to that described below for Lesotho.[32] The equilibrium between agricultural production and labor migration proved to be only transitory.[33]

One final factor which has been proposed as operating as a result of migrant labor, and which might serve to mitigate the labor shortages resulting from combining subsistence production and migrancy, is that of population growth. Joel Gregory and Victor Piché advance the interesting thesis that the migrant system contributes to a rapid rate of population increase, since high fertility is the household's response to its labor needs. In the typical African rural situation labor needs are high in the low-technology peasant and subsistence economies, and thus lead to high fertility, but labor market participation also encourages a high birth-rate, since the more laborers a household can field, the higher its income.[34] Not only migrant labor, but any expanding low-skill wage system where the costs of educating children are not high, might have this fertility effect.[35] From the household, village or even ethnic point of view, high fertility can indeed be an effective strategy under some circumstances, and labor migrancy may well have contributed to high population growth in Africa. But in the now common situation of limited available land, population growth will usually begin adversely to affect subsistence production.

Thus, Gregory and Piché go too far when they assert that 'given present conditions of development, the result of lower fertility might be greater impoverishment, famine, and perhaps even increased morbidity and mortality'.[36] What is rational at the household level is not necessarily so at the level of the nation or the capitalist system. With respect to the labor market, population growth retains its rationality only so long as the market is expanding and the costs of educating workers are not high. The main results of the contraction of the market in eastern and central Africa in the 1950s and in South Africa in the 1970s have been widespread unemployment and poverty. Today, 'credentialism' is making it harder for those without secondary education to obtain jobs. As the number of women, children and elderly in one family who are dependent on a single wage-earner expands, they eke out an existence in rural areas at great ecological cost and express their frustrations at great political cost. Without an expanding labor market or a socialist full-employment policy, high population growth can only pose great human risks.

Having examined some of the factors which can mitigate the possible negative effects on agriculture of the withdrawal of labor, we now turn to the question of whether migrant labor can stimulate, or at least coexist with, agricultural development beyond simple subsistence production. The question is what happens to the new cash the migrants bring home with them – is it invested productively in agriculture? Much obviously depends on the size of the income remitted to the rural areas, and in Africa the low wage levels for most migrant workers have not been such as to furnish much impetus for rural development. In general, though, the strategy of using migrancy to generate cash for agricultural investment does not appear to be very often successful. Rempel and Lobdell, for example, review an extensive literature on remittances in a number of African and Asian countries, and conclude that consumption and educational expenditures predominate, with remittances serving largely to maintain the existing level of rural living rather than to stimulate agricultural development.[37] The reason, it has been argued, is that, being rational economic actors, migrants tend to come from areas of inherently low development potential. Whether this is so or whether, as is more likely, the migrants come from areas which have been actively underdeveloped, migrancy does not usually seem to have provided the basis for a self-sustaining rural development independent of other changes in the rural environment such as, for example, the market for a given rural product. Migrancy can be a successful strategy, though, for individuals operating in favourable contexts.

In addition to these external reasons for the lack of rural development, there are also causes internal to rural society. Among African groups first entering the labor market, rising bride prices were a widespread phenomenon and often served the latent function of bolstering the faltering incomes of the older generation at the expense of the young male workers. Harries has described this situation among the Tsonga of Mozambique in the 1880s, maintaining that most of the new wages circulated unproductively among the *numzane* or elders. When wages were converted to *lobola*, they took on a social rather than a market value. Often the sterling was kept in trust, and could not be invested or 'eaten' in the expansion of agricultural production. Sterling was thus 'encapsulated' in a separate circuit of exchange, and most of the development potential of the migrants' wages was neutralized. Cadets were thus doubly exploited, by the mine masters at work and by the elders at home.[38]

In this formulation the lack of impact of the migrants' wages has been attributed to social structure rather than to ecological or technical conditions. The power of the elders is seen to be the key factor. In other cases, it is probably equally likely that lack of any other profitable investment options was just as important. The Kenya Maasai, for example, and many other cattle-keeping groups, invested nearly all their wages in cattle. Cattle were the traditional means of accumulation, the self-reproducing store and symbol of wealth. In pastoral societies cattle supplied nearly all nutritional and clothing needs, including dung for fires and hut-building, and could be exchanged for wives. With enough cattle men needed nothing else. It is only from the capitalist point of view that accumulation of cattle, without the aim of selling them or any of their products on the open market, is irrational. It was perfectly rational given the social system of the pastoralist. It is a matter of some controversy whether such systems persisted so long because their members chose them or because of various colonial prohibitions on the upgrading of African cattle and dairy products to enable them to bring good prices. In any event, most of the cattle accumulators were indeed left behind in the rush to acquire the new commodities of Western capitalist society.

Where cash-crop production developed in Africa, it was most often in spite of, or as an alternative to, labor migration, rather than as a consequence of it. It often happened that cash crops developed in an area that was simultaneously exporting labor. The effect was not necessarily a decrease in labor migration – contrary to the prediction of most colonial administrators and settlers, who objected to African peasant production. As Elizabeth Colson pointed out for the Plateau Tonga, the successful development of cash crops only temporarily inhibited labor migration; in the long run artificial and natural limits on the arable land available led to a reemergence of migration. When the Tonga developed a market for their crops in the late 1920s and early 1930s, there was a drastic fall in migration. Even though land quickly became scarce in some areas, in the western part of their reserve new fields could be opened up. But by the 1950s most of the usable land had been taken up, and people had either to migrate permanently to the north toward Lusaka or to go out temporarily to work. After 1950 there was a steady increase in migrant labor.[39]

The most significant factor making for the continuation of labor migration may not be simply land limitations, but rather the emergence of rural stratification. This was the case in the Kiambu area of southern Kikuyu in Kenya before 1945. Here the population density was high, and land limited; but the area was also fertile and near to Nairobi and other white settler markets. Relatively permanent out-migration as 'squatters' on to European estates was high, as was participation in circulatory migrant labor, but peasant cash-crop production also increased. The result was rural stratification: those who could accumulate through wage labor or education or as chiefs bought up the lands of the poorer. By the 1930s the lineage or *mbari* structure of joint landholding had begun to disintegrate in favor of individual ownership. Chiefs, headmen, elders, teachers in mission schools and other educated government employees such as clerks bought the land of the less fortunate. As time went on access to training broadened, and anyone who could get a white-collar, artisan or semi-skilled job – as, for example, a mason, lorry or taxi driver, or domestic servant – could then translate those wages into planting of cash crops in the rural area, relying on his wife and hired workers to perform the labor. Some of the large landholders became 'progressive farmers', marketing black wattle and improving cattle and milk production in the 1930s. But their enterprises were held back by repressive state policies and, as a result, they often maintained both a labor market position and rural enterprise. The poor, on the other hand, were more and more forced into unskilled, poorly paid labor market positions and were not able to save enough to develop, or even sometimes to retain, their landholdings.[40]

Here we see a distinctive pattern of double participation, of very active involvement in both wage labor and rural marketed production, of 'straddling'. In this case the inequities in the labor market *reinforced* those in the rural area, and labor participation *contributed* to the development of cash crops. After Mau Mau, land access among the Kikuyu increased, but today they broadly continue their dual pattern. Stays in the labor force have lengthened to include almost the whole of a man's adult life, but farms are managed in various ways, either by short visits at weekends or by resident wives and hired laborers. The number of those who are both land-poor and underemployed, on the other hand, has grown significantly. The success of this pattern depends a great deal on the fortunate location of the Kikuyu near to labor markets, local produce markets and transport links to export markets. Groups further from the commercial centers find it more difficult to combine crop sales and wage labor, since costs of transport and farm management increase.

In contrast to the patterns in Ghana and Nigeria, the Kikuyu never experienced a period of exclusive reliance on the growing of export crops. As peasants, the Kikuyu were always constrained by the presence of the white settler economy, yet they were never quite eliminated by it. The larger farmers were the ones to suffer the most from such policies as the prohibition of African coffee-growing and the restrictive quality control on beef, butter, milk and maize. The majority of Kikuyu therefore remained 'middle peasants', and even today the large farm sector, now partly African, is a dominant part of the economy. For the poor and middle peasantry, labor migration in this case serves valuable functions as an escape valve for excess population and as a source of new capital for modest investments.[41]

The most successful cases of independent African farmers producing for the export market are found in West Africa, but even here they have not been able to ignore the labor market entirely. Even when such farmers do not themselves take up wage employment, one common pattern is for them to invest in education for their sons and daughters, enabling these to enter the labor market on the level of white-collar, salaried and professional workers. This has been common in Nigeria. Or the farmer may have used earnings from a previous period of employment to invest in the farm, or he may turn back to migrant labor when crop earnings fail, as in Ghana. Still another pattern is found in the southern Cameroon, where cocoa incomes have remained higher than the income from most wage jobs. Many young men migrate only temporarily, until such time as they can inherit the cocoa land, marry and return to farming.

Migrants and the rural economy

The inheritance may not actually be possible until the death of the father.[42] Finally, where there are inequalities of wealth in such rural situations, it tends to be poorer households, often those of in-migrants from elsewhere, who most quickly turn to further labor migration. Cases from Ghana and Nigeria will illustrate this.

In southern Ghana, cocoa-farmers have turned to labor migration in periods when their incomes from farming have been on the decline, while in periods of prosperity they have invested in the education of their children. In the village of Tsito in the Ewe area of south-eastern Ghana, Jette Bukh found that, as a consequence of the inflow of money from cocoa production in the 1920s, new investments were made in two directions: house-building and children's education. The first generation of educated young people acquired jobs in the civil services as administrators and teachers, as well as in the army and police. Their status rose in the community, they brought home money and increased political influence for their families, but they tended to move their place of residence permanently out of the village.

Over time the number of out-migrants has varied directly with incomes from cash cropping. In Tsito a large upswing in labor migration took place in the mid-1950s, when new land suitable for cocoa first began to become scarce. Earlier, young men had migrated temporarily in order to get cash to buy land, but by the 1950s new land for cocoa was impossible to buy and young men had to migrate anyway. Cocoa prices peaked in 1956–7 and began a long downward slide; a sharp fall in the mid-1960s led to another large increase in migration. By then migration had come to function as an alternative to the cash crop rather than as a supplement. In 1968 between one-half and two-thirds of the men aged 15–39 had migrated. Since then migration has continued to increase, many migrants even traveling beyond the borders into Nigeria as the rapid inflation of the 1970s undercut rising cocoa prices. As the Ghanaian economy has stagnated, in stark contrast to the boom in oil-rich Nigeria, the Tsito village has seen general impoverishment.[43]

In western Nigeria, on the other hand, the prevailing pattern has been 'accumulation without proletarianization', and the recent development of off-shore oil resources has reinforced this pattern. One prime route of accumulation has been cocoa-farming, but the oil boom is now leading to a disinvestment in agriculture. This has not meant an increase in labor migration, however, but rather self-employment in the tertiary sector, primarily in distribution and services. In the two Yoruba cocoa villages southeast of Ife studied by Sara Berry in 1978–9, many of the farmers had acquired the farms some years before from previous periods of wage employment or petty trade. They were originally in-migrants from the savannah area and maintained ties with their home villages there. The profits were not only reinvested in cocoa, but, since cocoa was seen as only one of a number of possible strategies of accumulation, most farmers also diversified into trade and, as in Ghana, invested in education for their children.[44]

Their strategies of diversity and mobility were just as evident in the period of declining farm income in the 1970s. Even though cocoa prices were rising, inflation was overtaking the cocoa proceeds, and in addition the cost of rural farm labor was rising even faster than cocoa prices, as workers streamed into towns to pursue better opportunities there. So the farmers as well moved out of cocoa into trade, craft or other self-employed service occupations. And the number who were sending one or more of their children to secondary school had more than doubled in the decade before 1979. Those who could not afford post-primary schooling almost invariably apprenticed their sons and daughters to traders, artisans or other small-scale non-agricultural entrepreneurs. Two common occupations for children of farmers were as teachers and as self-employed mechanics.

Even those who had previously worked as agricultural laborers have tended either to become farmers themselves or to leave for tertiary self-employment, contributing to the farmers' labor supply problems. Cocoa does not need large labor inputs, and most farmers have relied heavily on family labor, but problems of labor supply and wages have undercut their efforts to expand. As Berry puts it, employers cannot hope to attract labor merely in exchange for daily subsistence. The thousands of petty traders, artisans and casual workers who make up the bulk of the urban (and much of the rural) labor force act not so much as a 'reserve army of the unemployed', but rather as a pool of would-be accumulators who attach themselves to a particular master or patron only if he or she is likely to help them become economically independent in the long run.[45] In general, capitalist development in western Nigeria has not created a substantial number of dispossessed or proletarianized people. Most Yoruba have been able to realize a measure of economic prosperity, and have not been forced to work for others for long periods of time. This trend toward self-employment has tended to reinforce communal and descent group solidarity, which undercuts class-based forms of action.

Western Nigeria may represent a limiting case in the spectrum of possible combinations of farming and wage work in Africa. Established farmers often combine farming with another occupation, but that alternative is either self-employment or white-collar work. In general it would seem that, the better one's income from farming, the better one's children's chances in the full-time labor market.

At the other end of this spectrum lie the cases of extreme rural poverty where the rural population has become almost completely dependent on oscillating migrant labor.

Present-day Lesotho in southern Africa, studied by Colin Murray, illustrates this situation.[46] In this area the factors that, in the cases of the Mambwe and the Mossi, served to guarantee the survival of subsistence production have failed. The necessity of engaging in long work contracts has prevented the institutionalization of a seasonal pattern; the generally low wages increase the length of time spent in the work force; competition from state-supported European farmers and a state-imposed embargo on grain exports have had a strong negative impact on agriculture; and the ecological situation is relatively unfavorable although not insurmountable.

The Sotho today search for work in a completely different context from that of the Mambwe or the Mossi in the 1950s. First, the market for skilled and unskilled labor, which is largely in South Africa, is not expanding but contracting. Second, rural poverty is such that a great many people would undoubtedly have already migrated to towns or elsewhere were it not for the enforcement by South Africa of strict pass laws, temporary contracts and prohibitions on permanent town residence for most Africans. The situation in rural Lesotho today is therefore somewhat artificial, a construct of the South African policy of labor-repressive industrialization supported by the ideology of apartheid.

The most striking thing about rural Lesotho today is not the shortage of male labor, as among the Mambwe or Mossi, but the high levels of unemployment. The predicament of the Basotho is summed up in the universal and bitter complaint *mosebetsi ha o eo*, 'there is no work'.[47] Lesotho is formally an independent nation, and since the 1960s Basotho as 'foreigners' have been legally excluded from all sectors of the South African labor market except mining and agriculture. Still, the main efforts of men are devoted not to agriculture but to expanding their labor-market experience so as to make themselves more marketable. However, their access to this market is becoming increasingly precarious, as South Africa attempts to attract more internal labor to the mines and to externalize the bantustans.

Between 42% and 44% of the males aged 20–59, and between 51% and 52% of those aged 20–39, are absent from Lesotho at any one time, according to the census, but the actual rate of absenteeism may be even higher. Only a small percentage of women is absent, since entry into South Africa for work is illegal, but a few women do find clandestine work as domestic servants, and some find jobs within Lesotho itself.[48] The great majority of the men are engaged in mining, primarily gold- and coal-mining in the Transvaal, Orange Free State and Natal. The average Basotho man spends from 13 to 16 years working outside, on contracts of from 12 to 24 months. Men return for periods of rest between contracts, but the majority are able to take up a new contract within six months of returning home. Perhaps 27,500 are employed inside the country itself and about 200,000 migrants are employed in South Africa.[49]

Nearly two-thirds of all households in the village studied by Murray have a wage laborer in them, and the remaining one-third are relatively disadvantaged economically, even if they previously had one. Only if they can send out another migrant after the eldest male, usually the father, retires can they avoid poverty. About 70% of mean rural household income is derived from migrant earnings and only about 6% from crop production. Thus the actual distribution of wage laborers between households is the most important single variable determining a household's income and also its capacity to invest in agriculture and other economic activities. Small, female-headed households are particularly disadvantaged. One 1976 study found that at least three-quarters of all rural households had an income that could be defined as below poverty level.[50]

Why do the Basotho not invest more in agriculture?

Many observers have remarked on their attitude of listlessness and pessimism in this regard. Even the wage increases of the 1970s did not seem to bring a commensurate increase in agricultural inputs. In part this situation must be seen against the background of their economic history, which is a classic example of enforced decline. In 1867 the discovery of diamonds in the northern Cape Colony began the first major mineral boom in South Africa, and it provided a good market for Basotho crops, to which they responded with zeal and success. Exports of maize, wheat, sorghum and wool expanded, as did imports. From the 1880s, however, agriculture began to decline. Economic depressions, drought and population expansion all took a toll. When the gold boom began in 1886 in the Witwatersrand, Basotho grain was excluded by import prohibitions and by competition from American and Australian grain. The 1896 rinderpest epidemic wiped out 90% of the cattle. Competition from white farmers in the Orange Free State further reduced grain markets. World War I meant high prices for wool and grain again, and exports rose, but the depression of the 1930s was disastrous and coincided with an exceptional drought. After that time, as the South African market for labor grew, great increases took place in the numbers of Basotho who migrated out for work, and agriculture continued to decline.

Even today successful farming in Lesotho is a high-risk undertaking, subject to climatic vicissitudes and requiring a fairly large investment in cash, labor time and social relationships. Very few households are self-sufficient in the needed resources of land, oxen, ploughs and labor. In 1970 only 35% of families owned a plough, and over 50% owned no livestock at all. Hence cooperative arrangements were crucial in order to get land ploughed, but these did not always suffice. Ploughing must be done during a brief period in October and November, and it requires male labor, since it is hard, heavy work even with oxen. Thus, in the village Murray studied some 22% of the fields went uncultivated even in the relatively good year of 1972.[51]

It appears to be very difficult in this situation to combine agriculture and migrant labor, and most Basotho do not get over the critical threshold to successful farming. Even with wage increases they have found it easier simply to purchase more food. Still, agriculture retains a crucial 'residual security function', and nearly all migrants do invest in it in a small way, primarily in small livestock. The Sotho thus illustrate a situation of proletarianization without urbanization or even full-time wage employment.

§ 3 §

MIGRATION AND THE AFRICAN HOUSEHOLD

Labor migration cannot be fully understood without reference to its function within the household and extended family. In the African countryside the household is still the central unit of production as well as reproduction. Given this reality, it makes little sense to think of the migrant as an atomized individual decision-maker maximizing his or her personal income, as noted in Chapter I. Such an assumption might be somewhat closer to social reality in Euro-American societies, where the domain of non-capitalized personal and family obligations has been reduced, but it is hardly tenable in Africa. This all-too-convenient economic fiction must be replaced with an analysis of the actual household production relations of which migrancy is a part.

These production relations are not necessarily 'traditional' today, but are usually still pre-capitalist. They are not only production relations, but also relations of reproduction, of the care and maintenance of human labor energy and the generational reproduction of the labor force. They are a complex of beliefs, values and practices, structured at bottom by the exigencies of production and reproduction. This chapter will argue that household relations are not only drastically affected by male labor migration; they themselves have an independent influence on the supply of labor, its composition, and its length of stay in the marketplace. Put in terms of the articulation of modes of production, the domestic mode of production/reproduction is now generally subordinate to the capitalist mode, but that does not mean that it is without influence on the capitalist mode. Its internal dynamic constrains the operation of the capitalist mode in certain definable ways.

In all African societies the most fundamental socio-economic unit was the extended household, which formed the lower rung of the wider political–economic system. Except for the hunting and gathering groups, whose band structure and mode of subsistence were not associated with elaborated kinship organization, most pre-contact African societies lived either from hoe or plough agriculture or from animal husbandry. The simpler the agriculture, the more likely the society was to be matrilineal, a system in which, in its pure form, a group of siblings form the core of the extended family, and control access to land and children. The women do not move away from their natal family to marry; rather, men marry in, and retain land rights only in, the village of their family of origin. The children of the union are considered to belong not to the husband, but to the woman's matrilineage, the woman's brothers often acting as 'social fathers'. The elder men in such families control the division and inheritance of land, but a woman's security of tenure and rights over her children are usually somewhat greater in matrilineal societies than in patrilineal ones. Perhaps half of all agricultural societies were matrilineal.

In patrilineal societies, which included most of the agriculturalists and all of the pastoralists, the woman has to leave her family of origin to marry into the husband's descent group. Her children are considered to belong to the patrilineage, and she has use rights, rather than ownership rights, to the land that her husband provides for her. Land and children are inherited only through males. In both matrilineal and patrilineal systems, a man's status depended not directly on his control over land, for that was not a scarce resource, but rather on his control over a) quantities of subsistence goods such as yams or cattle, and b) people—wives, children and other dependants such as clients and slaves. The central dynamic of accumulation in such societies was to build up the numbers of dependants through polygyny, high fertility, or captives in war. The greater the household labor force, the more land could be productively used and the greater the group's prosperity.

African societies, especially the patrilineal ones, have been variously characterized as exhibiting a 'domestic mode of production' (Claude Meillassoux),[1] a 'lineage mode of production' (Pierre-Philippe Rey),[2] a 'family mode' (John Caldwell)[3] and, most recently, a 'patriarchical mode of production' (Jeanne Henn, Nancy Folbre).[4] Limited space prevents a detailed examination of these conceptions here, but each theorizes the relation of elders to juniors, and men to women, in the African household. The merit of the latter formulation is that it includes the exploitation of women as part of the accumulative dynamic of the mode of production itself.[5] Using this approach, one can construct a simplified model of the typical African patriarchal household in which there are three basic socio-economic positions: the dominant elder or patriarch, the subordinate junior males, who are temporarily dependent but will one day attain the position of household head, and, in the base position of permanent dependants, women and slaves. Proponents of the concept of 'patriarchal mode' argue that the elders can be seen as expropriating measurable surplus-labor time from the other family members, that therefore these categories can be considered 'classes' in the Marxian sense, and that the household is a system of production.[6]

In general, the elder males in African households controlled the labor of junior males and women, and access to the major means of production, land. They managed the organization of agricultural production, deciding when and what to plant, and performed the necessary rituals to ensure productivity and fertility. Junior males performed military and agricultural labor for the patriarch, until he allowed them to marry, inherit land and begin their own households. Only after transferring a substantial surplus to the elders in the form of labor service could the young man become an elder in his own right. However, the patriarchal household was also part of a network of extended kin, the lineage, whose elders wielded influence in such decisions as marriage or land allocation. Women, as wives, daughters and slaves, performed the bulk of the agricultural and reproductive labor, providing domestic and sexual services and child care. They 'belonged' to the patriarch; they could be beaten, or given as payment for debts. Daughters were exchanged for bridewealth, and had little say in who they married. Widows could be inherited as wives by their husband's kin. Women often had some economic independence, for example through trading or the sale of excess produce, and often some separate ritual powers. But in general they were subordinate to men.

One example of labor inputs in an African household is provided by Henn, who estimates from ethnographic evidence for the Beti of Cameroon that in this case the elders performed approximately 5 hours of labor-time per week in the pre-colonial era, junior males approximately 20 hours, and women 46 hours, the average level of labor time expended being 33 hours. If the average is also taken to be the general level of consumption, it is clear that women put in more than they consumed, amd males less.[7] Such figures probably do not hold for all African societies, nor are they automatically translatable into generalizations about rights, power and status. But they do indicate that African households were not without strong internal stratification on the bases of age and sex.

THE IMPACT OF MIGRANT LABOR

The varying impacts of migrant labor must be assessed not simply on households as a whole, but on those in different structural positions within households. Within the parameters sketched above there are certainly wide variations in the domestic roles of elders, junior males, women and slaves in different African societies. But in assessing the impact of migrancy what is most striking is not the variability according to differing household structures and kinship systems, but rather the similarity of certain effects despite variations in pre-existing domestic relations.

The advent of migrant labor has had the following general effects.[8] (1) It has tended to strengthen the independence of junior males in relation to their elders, even though many colonial legal and political practices upheld the authority of elders. It was at first nearly always only junior unmarried males who migrated, although later migration became general among adult, but not elder, men. (2) The migration of junior males has meant a loss of male labor in agriculture for which women's labor has had to compensate. The result has usually been a change in the traditional division of productive labor between men and women, such that women have taken over tasks formerly defined as 'male'. This has usually meant an increase in the labor burden of women and – unless they are sent to school – children. (3) At the same time, not labor migration *per se*, but the growth of new towns and centers of employment administered by Europeans, has created a new, though limited, possibility of escape for those who suffered exploitation in pre-colonial society, primarily women and slaves. Voluntary female migration to towns has increased. This development illustrates not only the 'pull' of the towns but the 'push' of the patriarchal mode of production itself. The colonial authorities did little to encourage it and often helped elders try to prevent it. Slaves also left, but in this case the colonial powers, with varying speeds, specifically abolished slavery and provided protection, land and employment to ex-slaves. These losses of labor to the rural household put additional pressure on those who remained. (4) In some areas where cash crops were not well developed and men, even older, married ones, spent long periods of time in wage labor leaving cultivation to the wives, the wives by default have gained greater *de facto* decision-making powers over the organization of cultivation and the day-to-day management of the household.

The extent of these effects varies dramatically with the extent of migrancy and of the availability of cash crops as an alternative source of income. The exposition which follows, therefore, is organized according to the same three basic variations that were distinguished in the preceding chapter: the functioning subsistence economy, the cash-crop areas, and the depleted labor reserves. For each of these areas we examine the four processes of change just listed, except that the migration of women is discussed in Chapter 6.

In the classic 'balance' situation, where migrancy coexists with, but has not disrupted, subsistence production, the effects on the relations between elders and junior males are apparently somewhat mitigated. The South African cases of the Pedi, the Sotho and the Tsonga described in Chapter 1 illustrate how in the early phases of labor migration the possibility of independent action by junior males could be effectively contained by the elders for some time, through their control of bridewealth prices, their demands for a portion of the migrant's wages and their continued control over the allocation of land. At the same time, the individually owned earnings of the migrants, and the loss of their labor in the rural economy, did pose a threat, which stimulated the elders to impose controls. Gluckman, for example, noted with reference to the Zulu and Lozi of South Africa that the elders depended on and received gifts of money from the migrants, in return for which they retained land for them.⁹

Similarly, among the Mambwe described by Watson and the Mossi described by Skinner, an effective system of chiefly and elder control seems to have prevailed, though with some modifications. Among the Mambwe, bridewealth payments increased, and absorbed a good part of the money the juniors earned. Sons were expected to give cash gifts to their fathers in return for the provision of cattle for bridewealth. Still, young men were said to be able to marry at a younger age than in the past.¹⁰ As in most cases of heavy involvement in migrancy, migration did not stop upon marriage; adult men migrated as well. Men were able to marry between the ages of 19 and 25 after one or two labor trips, but they often had continuing bridewealth debts. Of the men aged 15–19, 24% were away; of those aged 20–29, 65% were away; of those aged 30–39, 33% were away; and of those aged 40–49, only 13% were away. Migration usually stopped after age 40, and a man was considered an elder.¹¹

Quarrels between the generations over inheritance of property, always a strong theme of Mambwe politics, were said to be increasing with the increase in inheritable property and the uncertainty as to how to deal with the earned portion of an estate. Disputes usually broke out between a deceased man's brothers on the one hand and his sons on the other, as to who would get what share of his titles, wives, children, cattle and other property, including unspent wages.¹²

Among the Mossi, elders appeared to be retaining women longer, alleging that the young men 'do not deserve wives because they do not remain at home to help their elders perform the tasks that ultimately bring wives'.¹³ Since the Mossi do not have the institution of bridewealth, a young man cannot 'buy' a wife. So unless he is 'given' a wife after performing labor service, his only option is to 'steal' one from the elders or other men who have them. Migrant labor has given them increased resources with which to entice women in this way. Even prior to migration runaway wives were a problem for elders, because their attempt to monopolize young women conflicted with the dislike of the young women for older husbands. But with labor migration 'stealing' seems to have increased, and therefore young women, too, have more options.

Both Watson and Skinner report pressure from women for men to take them along to town, even for short periods, and also a new independence for women in the choice of marital partners.[14] Skinner writes that the days when a Mossi woman would resignedly accept an unhappy marital situation with the statement 'What can I do? My father sent me to sit here!' are gone. Now a woman can simply run away with a migrant, and is only too happy to enjoy the experience of travel. The relatives of the deserted husband can take no immediate action, and when the couple later returns they usually acquiesce, since French and now Upper Volta law supports the right of a woman not to be forced to marry or to remain with a husband against her will. The returning couple can often even keep the children born to them, since the traditional Mossi conception that all a woman's progeny belong to the man who first married her was also negated by French law.[15]

Even though the migration of junior males, together with new colonial laws, gave Mossi and Mambwe women more options within the marriage system, there seem to have been relatively few who migrated to town on their own, or on a permanent basis.[16] This in spite of the fact that in both cases there has been an increase in the agricultural labor burden on the household, presumably resulting in increased labor inputs by women, who in Mossiland now sell cooked food along the roadways to migrants, to raise cash. The elder household heads, however, still organize much of the subsistence cultivation among the Mossi.[17]

Where male labor migration led to greater stress on the food production system, women often had to adopt new agricultural strategies, take up new roles such as trading, or take over men's agricultural roles in order to ensure an adequate family income. This may take place despite the continued control of elders over marriage and land allocation. Such is the case among the Luo of western Kenya described by Margaret Jean Hay and Achola Pala Okeyo. Though patriarchal constraints on women still persist, married women, especially mothers-in-law and senior wives, who have authority over other women, have often become *de facto* farm managers.[18]

By the mid-1930s in the main Luo province of central Nyanza, some 36% of the able-bodied adult men were reported to be away at any one time, and almost all men to be engaged in migrant labor at some time in their lives. The contribution of wages to incomes was high: almost two-thirds of estimated total income was accounted for by wages in 1936. At the same time, population was increasing on a fixed land base.[19] Women coped with this situation in various ways: as one response, they moved more into trade and marketing, in which they had not been active previously. As agriculture became more intensive and double-cropping more common, to compensate for declining yields due to declining soil fertility, there ceased to be seasonal slack periods to which migrants could adjust their work schedules. Since more men were migrating, women had to take up the increased labor burden, and they did so by adopting labor-saving innovations and by reinvesting some time in trade.

Those whose husbands' wages were high enough hired male labor, such as ploughing teams, but most had to be content with other strategies. They increased the planting of cassava, since it required less labor and was more drought-resistant, and they adopted white maize, which matured more rapidly than sorghum and permitted two crops a year, whereas sorghum could only be grown during the long rains. They adopted improved hoe blades, hand- or water-powered grinding mills, and ox-drawn ploughs, bought with either the husband's wages or the wife's trading profits. They raised only enough staples for subsistence, then put other time into cash crops or market crafts such as pots, pipes and reed mats. The overall effect between 1930 and 1945 was to maintain agricultural output despite decreased labor inputs.[20]

A recent survey in 1974–5 confirms that many women are doing tasks formerly done by men, such as clearing bush, ploughing by themselves, and even constructing granaries, although in the majority of cases these tasks are still done by the husband with the help of hired labor. Women have formed work groups which hire themselves out for such tasks as weeding, and cooperative labor exchanges between households for weeding, harvesting and transporting crops from the fields are common. With the exception of the three tasks mentioned above, all the remaining farm tasks of hand-digging, planting, weeding, harvesting, transport and storage are done almost solely by the women themselves, indicating that they still bear a heavy work-load.[21]

One function of women for men which ironically became more important in all agricultural societies with the onset of labor migration and land limitation was that, in using and occupying land, a woman effectively established her husband's or son's claim to the land in customary terms. Whereas in pre-colonial property systems land rights were often a secondary issue in inheritance, since land was easily available, land rights assumed increasing importance in the colonial era. Hay has pointed out how labor migration among the Luo increased the need for a wife to remain on the land and use it, warding off potential claims to the parcel by other male relatives. It was partly for this reason that Luo elders strictly enforced customary marriage laws and strongly opposed women's migration to the towns.[22] Jane Guyer has pointed to the same phenomenon for the present-day Beti of southern Cameroon, a cocoa-farming area. Under conditions of land shortage, boundaries are difficult to defend against encroachment by kinsmen unless the land is actively worked. Therefore unmarried absent sons often depend on the continued cultivation by their widowed mother of the family lands after the death of the father, to hold their claim while they are away at wage labor.[23]

This function of women is only operative where land rights are still allocated through elder patriarchs. Where the capitalist pattern of individualized land tenure and registration of freehold titles has been adopted, not only the power of elders is undermined, but also the place-holding role of women. In this way the security of their access to the land is threatened. The switch to individual land tenure took place in many areas during colonial times, but only recently among the Kenya Luo. Pala Okeyo points out that there it compresses the developmental cycle of the household by prematurely identifying which portions of land go to which junior males. Hence for many years the Luo elders opposed such a transition. At the same time individual tenure confers the right to sell land to the highest bidder, a right which in all traditional systems was constrained in some way or other by lineage interests. As poor African men have been pushed into selling, their wives have been deprived of land. Since land titles are not usually given to women in these 'land reform' efforts, and since there is no new legal guarantee other than 'custom' that a man must provide land for his wife or widowed mother, some women are going to lose even their former tenuous access to land.[24] On the other hand, individualized tenure does open the way for those few women who have prospered through trade, wage-earning or prostitution to buy land directly.

The development of cash crops has tended in general to strengthen or at least maintain elder control over the younger generation. This is less true in areas with extensive wage-earning opportunities for young men, more true where migrant earnings are lower. Cash crops tend to sustain the elders' income, and they usually retain the right to allocate a valuable resource, land. Among the Beti in Cameroon the abolition of slavery during the colonial period deprived the elders of a good deal of household labor, at the same time that taxation and cash-crop cultivation increased labor demands. Henn estimates that the labor time of elders increased from about 5 to about 17–25 hours a week in the colonial era, reflecting the greater labor demands on the household and the reduced number of dependants, while the household labor time of male dependants rose from about 20 to about 49–55 hours a week in 1924–34, and that of women rose from 46 to 62–71 hours.[25] As against other areas of cocoa growing, in-migration of other peoples to supply hired labor was here not an important factor.

To allow a son to marry and set up his own household was both to lose access to his labor and to share the now limited land with him. It also meant a cash expense in the form of bridewealth. Therefore elders prolonged the period before allowing sons to marry and inherit land, and cadets became less certain of their eventual emancipation. In the face of such pressures young men began to engage in temporary labor migration to European plantations and forestry operations, to earn cash for bridewealth. But migration did not provide a complete escape for juniors, since wages were such that although a bride price might be saved up, a wife could never be supported outside the rural areas.

Only by gaining access to land could young men assure their prosperity, but, increasingly, most only returned to their natal village to do so at the death of their father. Even in 1973, for example, in one rural department north of Yaoundé, the majority of migrants had first left the village at age 15–20 and stayed in town an average of six years. Some 43% had returned home due to their father's death and would presumably remain, while 57% would probably migrate again.[26]

Whether the development of cash crops increases the labor burden of wives depends on the success of such development: where the husband's total income is great enough to allow for a heavy reliance on hired labor, the wife's manual labor contributions might be reduced, in favor of the farm management functions of a 'second-in-command'. More commonly, where incomes are smaller the woman's labor input almost always increases, since she is not only left with full responsibility for the food-crop production, but is often expected also to work on the cash-crop fields managed by her husband, perhaps in return for small gifts. In both cases, the pre-cash crop division of labor between men and women will have been disrupted, men typically reducing their roles in food production to specialize in cash crops, and women expanding the range of food-related tasks they undertake. At either level of income, if the husband is a full-time farmer she may remain a subordinate decision-maker on the farm (though she may, as in the case of the Yoruba, have an independent trading business), whereas if he is absent at wage labor for long periods she may gain a good deal of actual decision-making power in the domestic arena.

A partial exception to these generalizations occurs where men have traditionally specialized in food production and women in transport, processing and trade, as among the Yoruba in western Nigeria. Here cocoa cash cropping was simply added into the male farming system, and male hired labor was extensively employed. Women helped to some extent with the farm work, but their main contribution to increasing family incomes lay in expanding their trading networks. Here women can become more enterprising and more mobile than women who have been socially defined as responsible for all family food production.[27] In this case the introduction of cash crops intensified the pre-colonial sex division of labor, widening sex divisions along lines that were already etched in the preceding system.[28]

The Kikuyu, with their diversity of income levels and their combining of cash crops with wage labor, provide more typical examples of the changes cash crops may make in women's roles. Prior to European conquest, women provided a large portion of the subsistence labor. By the 1950s, as a result of labor migration, women were doing more 'men's work', such as clearing new land and caring for and milking cattle, increasing their labor burden.[29] By the 1960s the addition of cash crops such as chickens, eggs, milk, coffee and tea had substantially changed the nature of tasks to be performed, as well as to some extent the *de facto* division of labor between men and women. The normative or 'ideal' conception of the sexual division of decision-making has changed far less than the actual division, however. The normative conceptions are still that men are expected to dominate the domains of livestock, property transfers, all decisions on cash crops, disposition of income from cash crops, and socialization of school-age or initiated sons. Women's ideal decision-making domains include disposition of the proceeds from chickens and subsistence crops and disciplining of other children. In practice, though, women exercise strong decision-making power in daily decisions having to do with cash crops, and with the socialization of older sons, in addition to the areas in which they were 'ideally' to have power.[30]

Greet Kershaw's 1962 survey of four southern Kikuyu villages illustrates how the social roles and decision-making positions of women vary according to the extent of cash cropping and labor migration.[31] Some 57% of the families were poor, with little or no land (though some were young and stood to inherit land), 29% had land adequate to grow basic foods and a few cash crops, and 14% were well-off, with seven or more acres of land. In the first group, both husband and wife have to work for wages whenever possible, the men mostly in urban areas, where they often hold insecure and poorly paid jobs. Women take low-paid seasonal work on European coffee plantations or local farms. The wife is still, as was traditional, regarded as responsible for feeding the family, but finds that the means for doing so have greatly decreased. The husbands, being poor, have little or no influence in extra-domestic arenas, such as elders' councils or village rituals, and even within the household there is little disposable income to make any decisions about. Most have no cash crops, cannot think of acquiring more land. Their absence at work leaves most day-to-day household decisions to the wife. By comparison to the pre-colonial period, the man's status has been reduced, whereas the wife's has increased. These effects are similar to those found in 'labor reserve' economies generally, as described below.

Among the middle group with adequate land, the husbands also migrate for work, but more often to semi-skilled jobs with greater security and higher wage levels than among those in the poor category. Some savings may be accumulated over the years; these are invested in land, in cash crops and in education for the children. Land is seen as the most critical commodity, since the husband expects to retire and live from it. The wife's work-load on the land may be large, and the family may not be able to use all the land, renting some out to poorer families. The husband may demand that the wife work on his cash crops, in addition to her subsistence crops, but if she does she may gain a limited influence over the disposition of the proceeds, as a result of his absence at work. If she can work for wages, she is usually allowed to dispose of this income herself, though much of it usually goes on family necessities. For this category Kershaw suggests that there is some continuity with the traditional division of decision-making between husband and wife, but in fact the addition of male-dominated cash crops has considerably changed the situation.

In the third category are those who are active, expansion-oriented farmers, buying and improving land, planting cash crops, experimenting with new crops, developing their breeding stock of cattle. At the same time, true to the Kikuyu pattern, almost all the men are also employed, usually in white-collar occupations such as teaching and the civil service. In addition, they often operate various businesses. Many of them are able to be employed right in the local area, so that they can also effectively supervise their farms. They invest heavily in education for their children. Their wives are not employed, but are often prominent in community affairs. Their main task, however, is to be the husband's farm manager, to oversee the hired labor, to execute the husband's decisions. Reliance on hired labor relieves them of much of the actual farm labor. There may be some truly joint decision-making in these families, and many husbands seem to take their wife's agricultural expertise seriously. But by and large the women here seem to have lost a good deal of their independence by comparison to traditional times. Though they still maintain subsistence food production, that contribution is now a much smaller portion of the total family income. To some extent these women's subordinate domestic role is compensated for by an active, often leadership, role in women's community affairs, which have become an important force in

Kikuyu rural politics. This well-off category is a minority in Kikuyu society, however, by far the more common patterns being those found in the first two groups.

Where men were not engaging in migrant labor so extensively as the Kikuyu at the time of the adoption of cash crops, women have not been able to encroach as much on men's spheres of decision-making. In these cases the effect of cash cropping alone on the division of labor and decision-making can be seen more clearly. Men commonly withdrew from food production to concentrate on export crops, leaving women to take up the slack. Although men controlled the high incomes from the cash crop, women could diversify into small-scale market trade in foodstuffs. These trends are found among the Ewe in Ghana and the Beti in Cameroon.

Among the Ewe, women's independence from men in food production increased, but so did their responsibilities.[32] The Ewe inhabit a marginal cocoa area in the Volta region of southern Ghana. Cocoa was not grown on large tracts of land, as elsewhere, but was incorporated by local residents into smallholder subsistence production. In-migrants supplied some of the labor as employees or tenants (about 55% in 1973), but the immediate household supplied the rest. Before the adoption of cocoa, men were in charge of organizing food production and did a good deal of labor in it. Men and women both worked on the same household plots. For the staple crop, yams, men were responsible for clearing the land, digging the hills for planting, and cutting off the vine heads for replanting. Women did the weeding, planting and harvesting.

When cocoa planting was begun, food crops began to be relegated to less fertile land, since cocoa needed the rich humus of the forest area. Men worked more and more on the cocoa, and food plots were left largely to the women, who were not expected to help much with the cocoa. The marketing of the cocoa beans was also completely managed by men, the money from it being earmarked for either more investment in cocoa or house-building or children's education. Women's sale of food crops from family plots yielded some cash, but this money was used for the family and its disposition controlled by the male head. Women therefore began to establish their own separate plots in addition to the family one, from which they could sell crops and earn their own money.

A quite new and more separate division of labor thus emerged, although the returns to women's labor were much less. Whether their labor burden increased depended on how much hired labor could be afforded. One unambiguously negative effect has been a decline in nutritional standards, as the women have substituted cassava or maize for the traditional yams, these being less labor-intensive. Cassava, in particular, formerly a low-value 'hunger crop', is now the most widely planted food crop. It has a low nutritional value but grows well on the less fertile land they must now use. The amount of vegetables grown has also declined, and over-cropping and destruction of trees for charcoal have contributed to impoverishment of the land resources.[33]

Since the mid-1950s labor migration has increasingly superseded cocoa cultivation as the chief occupation of Ewe men.[34] This development has set in motion a new set of household trends, including a high percentage of female-headed households, both because of migrancy and because of a high divorce rate. Absentee males have meant that more responsibility, and presumably more actual decision-making power, have devolved upon women, as compared to the cocoa-boom years. Though burdened with feeding their families, women today have fewer resources with which to do so, and the situation has begun to approximate that in 'labor reserve' areas.

Farming appears to have been more exclusively women's work in the pre-colonial economy of the Beti in Cameroon than it was among the Ewe. Any work that involved handling the earth fell to women, including planting, weeding, and harvesting the traditional staple, yam. Men did work that involved wood or metal: hunting, trapping, tapping palm-wine trees, but also clearing the forest for planting, cutting yam stakes, building fences and storehouses and planting special supplementary crops that did not require the soil to be hoed before planting. As a man became an elder, his work input into farming declined, but his managerial control over such aspects of the production process as field size, length of fallow and fertility rituals increased.[35]

When cocoa cultivation was begun, it was done according to the techniques used for men's crops. Women's traditional obligation to provide harvest, processing and transport labor was extended to include cocoa, without any change in the cultural definition of the division of labor. There was little hired labor available to supplement. As in Ghana, in the early phases of cocoa-planting food crops could be interplanted with young trees, reducing the conflict between the food and export crop systems, but later the food crops had to be confined to separate plots tended almost exclusively by women. Today 84% of the total work put into food farming is done by women, a percentage that is larger than would have been the case in pre-colonial times. As happened among the Ewe, yam has given way to cassava and plantain as the major staples.

As among the Ewe, cocoa intensified the distinction between men's work and women's work, but in this case there were no new routes to female autonomy. Men moved into cocoa production; because of the crop changes and the decline of virgin forests and wild animals, their input into subsistence production decreased. But women have changed their work roles hardly at all by comparison to the

Ewe, since there is less scope in this area for expansion into food marketing and associated processing. As noted above, the work-load of both sexes has increased, especially that of women, so that food production could be kept up. But there is no evidence that the predominant role of men in decision-making about household income, including that generated by their wives, has changed.

Finally, we turn to the cases where labor migration and other economic forces have been so detrimental to the rural economy as to turn it into a poverty-stricken 'labor reserve'. In these cases the trends noted thus far in the relations between elders and juniors, men and women, reach their fullest development. The authority of the senior generation is greatly undermined, since the main resource they continued to control during the colonial era, land, has lost its former productivity. Wealth, in the form of wages, is small, and it is increasingly controlled by junior men. It can no longer be used to build up large households of many dependants, since it is not sufficient. Smaller households have become the norm, and they are units less of production than of consumption and reproduction. Older men can hardly ever build up large households through migrancy, as they would have in earlier times. As Murray puts it in the case of Lesotho men, 'Most must commit themselves in their declining years to dependence on the remittances of sons or of other junior kin who in their turn engage in the oscillating pattern.'[36]

With the decline of subsistence agriculture and the lengthy absences of men, the pre-migratory role divisions between men and women have quite thoroughly broken down. Women are now almost solely in charge of subsistence, though retired males and those between migrations give some assistance, mainly in ploughing. With respect to decision-making, it is unequivocally the case that the women's effective power has increased, given the high percentage of female-headed households, both because of absent husbands and because of the large numbers of divorced, separated and unmarried women. As for women's migration to town, both men and women aspire to wage employment, and in the southern African cases history suggests that, if South African law allowed it and if jobs were available, there would be a high rate of female migration to town.

In the Lesotho village of Ha Molapo studied by Murray in 1974, 70% of the households were effectively managed by women. They were divided between those headed by widowed, separated or unmarried women (44% of all households), and those whose male heads were absent migrants.[37] Similarly high percentages of female-headed households, in both senses, are found in other labor-exporting areas: in the Transkei the figure is 67%,[38] and among the Ewe it is 42%.[39]

These figures reflect the instability of marriage and the high rates of separation and divorce in these areas, as well as the shorter life-span of men compared to women. Long periods of conjugal separation appear to lead to conjugal breakdown. However, of equal significance for the assessment of the economic position of women is the number who effectively manage because the husband is absent working; too often he does not or cannot contribute adequately to the household's welfare. Bukh's findings are similar to Murray's: she emphasizes that 65% of all women over 18 in the Ewe village were almost solely responsible for the daily support of themselves and their children.

Household politics in Lesotho revolve around access to the migrant's wage, whether it is earned by the husband, son, father or even mother. As noted in Chapter 2, the number of migrants in a household is the single overriding factor determining that household's prosperity. Though women spend the majority of their time in agriculture and petty trade, these activities do not yield nearly the amount a wage does. Even the collective and community endeavors in which many women participate do not bring much return. By contrast to the enthusiastic energy called forth by women's cooperative self-help projects in rural Kikuyuland, such efforts in Lesotho lack state support and seem quite devitalized.[40]

Despite women's day-to-day management of the rural household, there is typically a disjuncture between their responsibilities and their power to fulfill them. Since the husband is the one who receives the wage, either at work or at home under deferred pay arrangements, he alone decides what portion to remit to his houshold, and frequently gives directions as to how it should be spent. Women frequently complain of inadequate remittances. In relatively well-off families, where a regular monthly remittance assures the wife of an acceptable level of security, the balance of authority is likely to remain with the man, but where husbands are considered irresponsible, or migrants are younger sons likely to spend money on women and drinks, women are pushed to assert themselves. Murray gives us the case of ᶜMaPuleng, whose husband had not only sent instructions for purchase of a table and chair when food was immediately needed for their three children, and hired labor needed to plough their only field, but also only sent small remittances and spent a good part of his last paycheck on a risky horse-buying scheme which failed. But she never flouted his wishes directly, only complained, feeling frustrated, bitter and depressed. She bought the cheapest table and chair she could find. ᶜMa Tau, on the other hand, was an elderly widow whose main cash income was from Esther, her deceased son's wife. Esther was employed as a domestic worker in Johannesburg, and ᶜMa Tau regarded her as the next head of the household. As for Felix, a young kinsman raised in the houschold who had recently taken his first contract at an asbestos mine, she appropriated all the money he brought back with him in order to stop him from 'wasting' it on drink and girls.[41]

Bridewealth payments continue to account for a significant proportion of income transfers in the reserves, and for a good part of migrants' wages. They are a very important, and in some cases almost the only, source of income for the senior (retired migrant) generation. Since they are enforceable in court, they are an effective way of insuring at least some income transfer from the juniors to the seniors and of preventing elder poverty.

But there has been an even more profound change in the function of bridewealth as compared to earlier times: it is now elderly women, just as much as elderly men, who can get access to it. Murray argues that whereas at one time *bohali* transactions represented bargaining conducted by men over the productive and reproductive powers of women, today they represent bargaining conducted by women over the earning capacities of men.[42]

This situation arises because of the large number of young people resident with their mothers only, or with their mothers' parents, reflecting the high rates of separation and divorce. In order to retain control of these children's earning capacities, the female household head typically attempts to repudiate the father's claims to the children, arguing that not enough bridewealth was paid to establish paternity. Many bridewealth disputes occur between the households to which individuals are attached by reason of residence and support and those asserting an alternative claim of paternity; they are thus inter-household conflicts over recruitment of the next generation. There are a very large number of households now where the lineal links are through the women only. In these conflicts women emerge as 'powerfully motivated and resourceful custodians of household integrity'.[43]

Migration and the African household

An illustrative case is that of ᶜMaNtsoaki, an old woman in Ha Molapo, who vigorously maintains that Thali, an old man in the village who 'married' her daughter Ntsoaki, never paid enough *bohali* to establish paternity over her granddaughter Lydia, who runs a successful medical practice in the Transvaal and who will shortly retire to Ha Molapo. Nor, more immediately, does he have claim to Lydia's son Teboho, who has a relatively secure job with a Johannesburg construction company. Thali would like to claim Teboho as his heir, and thus be entitled to support from him, but the enmity between him and the woman-linked family headed by ᶜMaNtsoaki – consisting of ᶜMaNtsoaki, Ntsoaki, Lydia (who was never married) and Teboho – is too great. Teboho himself could recognize and probably legitimate the claim by going to live with Thali and giving him some financial support, but he could not do this without reducing his contributions to ᶜMaNtsoaki's household and incurring their undying anger at being betrayed. ᶜMaNtsoaki's intransigence on the bridewealth issue has thus far prevented any loss to her household of Teboho's earning power.[44]

THE INFLUENCE OF THE HOUSEHOLD ON MIGRANT LABOR

It is apparent that capitalism and labor migration have tended to undermine the patriarchal African household in some ways and to strengthen it in others, depending on the particular form of the capitalist impact. But even though the family as a mode of production is dominated by the forces of capitalism, it is not wholly without influence on them. Both in their pre-colonial and in their changed colonial forms, the production relations of the household have affected several important features of the patterns of labor migration.

This impact has taken place in three main areas: a) the

composition and size of the labor supply to the capitalist economy; b) capitalist wage levels; and c) population growth. Whatever predictions one might make about the labor supply from a general examination of the state of the rural economy, its age and sex composition are not among them. To understand these characteristics of the labor force, one must turn to the structure of the household. In the case of junior males, women and slaves, their under-privileged position in the household would predispose them to take advantage of avenues of change, but the junior males initially had greater freedom to do so. To them, labor migration often seemed to offer the possibility of bettering their position within the patriarchal structure, hastening the day when they would accede to elder status. Also, the migration could be ended when sufficient wealth or status had been achieved. Male labor migration, then, emerged out of the latent conflict between junior and senior males.

The migration of women has been growing slowly throughout the colonial era and up to the present, as described in Chapter 6. That there has not been more of it is conventionally explained by the assertion that few wage opportunities have been available to them. But colonists and European investors in other parts of the Third World have commonly hired women as domestic workers and factory labor, for example in food processing in Asia and Latin America. The small number of women in the labor force in Africa must have a great deal to do with the nature of the pre-existing modes of production there, particularly with the important female role in subsistence farming, which was reflected in the household division of labor between the sexes. In this context, far from women being sent out to work by their fathers and husbands, as in Asian forms of patriarchy, African women often faced severe sanctions for attempting to migrate. Colonial political regimes usually supported the elders in this aspect of their traditional prerogatives, as described more fully below, and female migration often assumed the character of protest. On the other hand, the early objections of elders in many societies to the migration of junior males were silenced by forced labor, by taxation and by cooptation of chiefs. Thus, in Africa nearly all wage jobs until recently have been held by men, including domestic service, factory processing, clerical work, teaching and medical assistance. Since the 1950s, however, African women's participation in wage labor has been growing; in South Africa it has been growing steadily since the 1920s. This trend can be traced to the disintegration of the patriarchal household there.

In addition to its effect on the aggregate age and sex composition of the migrant labor force, it is more widely acknowledged that household composition affects the *incidence* of migrancy among families. A man who has many children, or with an elderly father or mother to support, may be more disposed to migrate than one who does not; the presence or absence of a wife's productive labor will also affect his decision. Murray cites a case in Lesotho of a man whose wife had died leaving four children. With no one to look after them, Motlalepula could not migrate. But the solution was equally clear: he must find another woman, either the grandmother or a new wife, to do the child-care work.[45]

The household may also affect the overall *rate* of migration, the aggregate labor supply, and also the work force's dependence on wage-earning and hence its exploitability.[46] Both these factors are of critical significance in capitalist development. Given that land is the chief alternative to wage labor, and that land rights are in many areas still refracted through the household, it is obvious that family arrangements of access and inheritance may affect whether any group is proletarianized and to what degree. A not-uncommon situation in Africa involves not the exclusion of some sons from the inheritance, which would have happened among the European peasantry, but rather the prolongation by elders of the time before the inheritance is transferred. The effect of this is to keep junior males in the labor force at frequencies that would not be predicted simply from comparisons of average rural and wage incomes. Henn has shown for the Cameroon that, even though average rural incomes were stagnant between 1964 and 1974, the urban wage level was lower and was actually declining. Yet, the migration of rural male youth to towns continued unabated. This effect cannot be explained without reference to the patriarchal household relations, which determined that sons must await their father's death before inheriting farms. The son who remained in the village, considering the surplus-labor extracted from him by elders, would have less possibility of achieving the average rural living standard than would the migrant, even at diminished urban wages.[47] It is not clear how widespread this effect is in Africa today, because in Ghana and southern Nigeria, where similar inheritance situations obtain, non-farm income options have been more attractive in recent years.

Finally, the subservient position of junior males and women in the household can affect not only the labor supply, but wages as well, in two ways. First, in those cases where junior male urbanward migration is traceable to rural household production relations, the build-up of an urban 'reserve army' of workers exerts a downward pressure on wages. More broadly, insofar as household structure affects the ability of the rural economy to be productive, it affects rural incomes in general, which then affect rates of migration and thus the level of urban wages. This leads to the second, and probably today the more widespread, way in which the patriarchal household affects urban wages, and that is through women's continued subsistence labor. As Wolpe and others have pointed out, where a large part of the care and reproduction of the labor force continue to be performed in the subsistence economy at no cost to the capitalist, the rural economy is subsidizing the capitalist, enabling the wage to cover only daily, not lifetime or generational, costs of reproduction.[48] It is the *patriarchal* (in a materialist sense) organization of the rural economy, expressed through the unit of the household, that determines that it will be women, and not men, who continue to perform these functions. Today as in the past, partriarchal control of women benefits the capitalist by subsidizing the migrant's wage.

The semi-independent dynamics of the patriarchal household may not always work in the capitalists' interest. The 'positive' effects of patriarchy for early capitalist development in Africa are found mostly in its functional articulation with the migrant labor system, after initial resistances had been broken. But there are also negative effects, and the articulation as a whole has to be seen as contradictory and dialectical.

One arena of potentially destabilizing effects is that of population growth. As Caldwell and others have argued, decisive effects on fertility flow from the 'household economy'.[49] As Seccombe puts it, various household forms have discrete 'fertility regimes', which are the result both of the distribution of power and the marriage rules internal to the household and kin group and of the external forces which determine the costs and benefits of having children and the availability – in both technical and cultural terms – of contraceptive technology.[50] We propose here that the particular fertility regimes which function in most African households today are the result of the specialization in cash crops and migrant labor, in varying combinations, together with patriarchal relations.

In those areas predominantly engaged in cash-cropping in pure form, the dynamic is similar to that prevailing among 'proto-industrial' or cottage industry households in Western Europe in the seventeenth and eighteenth centuries. These were households of family-organized production for commodity markets, and have been termed 'demographic hothouses' as a result of their high demand for family labor leading to high fertility. Only in periods of high incomes from the marketed commodity, which make possible the supplement of hired non-family labor, is the dynamic mitigated. Cash crops tend to preserve the authority of male household heads, as we have seen, and to confirm the flow of wealth from children to male adults; thus, from the male elder's point of view, the economic benefits of children far outweigh the small costs represented by what they consume or the labor of raising them. From the woman's point of view as well, though the physical and income costs of bearing children are higher, they are offset by the compatibility of child care and work in food and export crop production (the non-separation of the sites of production and reproduction), and by the positive labor contributions even young children can make to her total labor burden.

In African households primarily dependent on migrant wage labor the fertility regime is similar to that in early proletarian families in Western Europe, in that the demand for family labor is determined in the short term by the separate employment possibilities for men, women and children in the capitalist sector. Since in Africa, as compared to Western Europe, there have been relatively few wage opportunities for women and children, the calculation turns almost solely on opportunities for male labor, but the result still tends toward high fertility. Since there is little costly investment in the laborers' training or education, the household can produce marketable workers at a relatively low cost and has a strong incentive to produce as many as possible, since wages are low. Even for women in this situation, unless there are other income-earning avenues

Migration and the African household

available, there is relatively little opportunity cost to having children.

The result in both cases, and therefore in most parts of Africa, has been high birth-rates, which, combined with the declining mortality-rates, have produced rapid population growth. Theoretically, a divergence between these two patterns can be expected at times of falling crop prices and falling wages. In the cash-crop regime, if market prices fall the family must intensify production and so increase its fertility. In the wage-dependent situation, if wages fall the same logic might obtain, but if actual job opportunities contract, or cease to expand, it does not. In this situation, high fertility only contributes to further downward pressure on wages.

The continuance of high fertility among most African populations even in the face of stagnating employment must be related to only partial dependence on wages and to the continuing possibility in many areas of reverting to some level of subsistence or cash-crop production. As Caldwell suggests, the increasing necessity of educating children is the chief factor that will force a change in this situation, since it dramatically raises the cost of children as well as the quality of their labor power. The only segment of African populations where fertility is dropping is among fully proletarianized white-collar workers. The average number of children per woman in these families is in the neighborhood of 4 to 6, while in rural areas 10 to 12 is normal. Without government intervention, this pattern of the salaried elite and sub-elite may be extended to the entire population only at a much later stage of capitalist development.

§ 4 §

ENTERING AND LEAVING THE WORK FORCE

There are two dimensions which, more than any others, shape workers' consciousness and the strategies they choose to defend their interests in the work force. These are the character of their proletarianization – their relation to the wage labor market, as opposed to alternative ways of making a living – and the character of their work – that is, the direct social and technical relations of production. This chapter will focus on the first of these factors, and the next one on the second.

The term 'proletarianization' refers to the increasingly *economically necessary* character of participation in the wage labor market. The great majority of African workers, male or female, are proletarianized, in that alternative means of livelihood have gradually been closed off. As described in the preceding chapters, lands have been expropriated, and the income derivable from agriculture has in a number of ways been reduced. Even in generally prosperous agricultural areas, such factors as land shortage, erosion, poor weather and lack of technical assistance or credit may affect individual families adversely, forcing them into the labor market. In early years, direct physical force was at least as widespread as economic compulsion.

Proletarianization in Africa was a fitful, halting process, often as much unwanted by capitalists as by workers. Many early worker struggles – desertion to rural areas, resistance to recruitment and forced labor – were struggles *not* to become workers, to escape from or to retard the process. Capitalists, and more often colonial governments backed by settlers, or modern governments concerned about rural development, have also sought to limit the process, in the extreme case of South Africa by the draconian measures of denying Africans long work contracts or residence rights in urban areas. Despite such efforts, proletarianization in eastern, central and southern Africa turned out to be, quite broadly, a linear process, in most cases not easily reversible.

However, some wage labor participation also occurs from choice rather than from necessity. Potential workers who have some skills or resources which are usable in both the wage sector and the peasant sector will be able to exercise a genuine element of choice. Wherever urban wages are higher than peasant incomes, either on the average or in certain categories of occupation, many such workers will choose to try their luck in the labor market. For example, Paul Lubeck has described how recent migrants to Kano, Nigeria, are attracted by the opportunity to study Islamic texts while working in a factory; many of them make use of Koranic school contacts in adjusting to urban life and finding a job.[1] The pursuit of education (by those who can afford its opportunity costs) is an important motive in urban migration, since it holds out the possibility, if not the actuality, of upward mobility.

It is also increasingly the case that many of those forced into the labor market cannot actually find jobs. Analytically, therefore, we need to distinguish two sets of processes: a) those of separation from the means of production and from precapitalist labor controls, and b) those of incorporation into the wage labor force. The term proletarianization more nearly captures the first set of processes; for the second we propose to use the term 'conditions of incorporation'. The first process has been discussed in preceding chapters; the second will be treated here.

The conditions of incorporation into wage labor are determined by non-wage opportunities on the one hand, and employer offerings on the other. They include a) the other income-producing options open to the workers and how the potential income from them compares to wage incomes; b) the percentage of total income derived from wages; c) whether or not the worker is coerced; and d) whether the work is formally recruited and contracted, the length of the contract, and the prospects for remaining on the job for longer periods of time. All these are material, not psychological, factors; but each different situation has important implications for labor consciousness and action.

The terms on which the worker enters and leaves the paid labor force are too often overlooked in labor studies, since most of them focus on workers who are full-time and fully proletarianized. In the study of migrant wage-earning in Africa, however, examination of the conditions of incorporation is absolutely crucial.

Three general categories of incorporation can be distinguished in Africa today, corresponding broadly but not exclusively to the three kinds of rural economies discussed in Chapter 2. First, there are those workers who, either as individuals or as ethnic groups, have access to lands which are so impoverished that there is virtually no possibility of subsisting from agriculture or animal husbandry. They and their families are highly, if not exclusively, dependent on wage work for a living, even if they in fact have some access to land. Their rural condition cannot be expected to improve during their lifetimes through, for example, inheritance of more land. Many workers in southern African areas such as Botswana, Lesotho and the Transkei are in this category. They are proletarianized workers who, were it not for their lack of legal access to urban areas, the state-imposed 'tribal homeland' system and the time limitations on labor contracts, would probably not be migrants at all, but full-time workers. In these cases migrancy does not necessarily mean only partial proletarianization – a fact which goes far toward explaining these workers' increased propensity for labor militancy.

Second, there are workers who genuinely straddle the fence between wage and non-wage work, who invest effort and labor time (or that of their wives and children) in farming and who derive a significant proportion of their total household income from agriculture, whether as subsistence or as marketed commodities. Their participation in the labor market may vary according to the relative levels of cash-crop prices and wages. It may be on a short-term but recurrent basis, often on contracts of from six months to two years. Young men who go out to work for a number of years until they can inherit their fathers' land fall into this category. These are the classic 'migrant laborers', the semi-proletarianized peasant-workers. Their double interests in both the peasant and the wage economy lead to particular styles of labor protest, such as desertion to the rural area in the face of poor conditions or low pay, or acceptance of only short-term or seasonal work.

Third, there are those who participate full-time in the labor market, but primarily because they wish to, rather than because they have to. That is to say, their wage work brings them higher incomes than agriculture could, but they could still return to farming if it were really necessary. Usually it is only those who have been able to get access to education or training and who hold salaried, white-collar or particularly skilled and highly paid jobs who are in this position, although by no means all white-collar or skilled workers have land. Such workers usually spend most of their working lives at their job. Their incorporation into wage work is as complete as it is for those in the first category, yet in addition they have the option of investing in the peasant economy. And most of them use their discretionary income to do just that, buying houses, farm equipment, livestock and land, and maintaining social ties to community, politicians and extended family. Thus they are not proletarianized, in the sense of being separated from the rural means of production. On the contrary, if the distance of their job does not make it impossible, these workers may actually become successful farmers as well, succeeding in two arenas. In this they are similar to the straddlers in category two, but their rural success clearly depends on their wage income and would be impossible without it. Furthermore, they usually do not have the time to manage farms directly themselves, and must depend heavily on hired labor and extended family, which eats into profits. These workers, like those in category one, are dependent on the labor market and are active in militantly defending their interests as workers.

These three categories are meant to be merely a rough ordering of what is actually a great variety of relationships to wage labor in Africa. It would not be useful to attempt to delineate more rigidly these groupings or to try to put numerical dividing lines between them. A more formal set of categories might be derived from specifying in greater detail the two different sets of production relations, wage and non-wage, in which the workers are involved. In such a model, individual decisions based on these production relations would determine the aggregate supply of labor. Employer decisions would determine the demand for labor. The supply and demand condition prevailing in any given area is a discrete factor in itself, and one which has a great effect on workers' bargaining strategies in the labor market and on their probability of success.

In sketching the three types of incorporation, it was assumed that an individual made a decision to offer himself

Entering and leaving the work force

for work based on the prevailing economic situation. In the history of the development of wage labor in Africa, however, there was too often no possibility of individual decision: legal forced labor and recruitment systems which depended on clandestine coercion were widespread. The rest of this chapter describes these systems and African reactions to them.

FORCED LABOR

The component of sheer physical force in the development of an African working class was large, particularly in the settler and mining areas of eastern, central and southern Africa. Since about 1945, however, many elements of direct coercion have declined in most parts of the continent. In early years in all areas, Africans were legally subject to a certain amount of forced labor to be used on public works projects; in addition there was the *sub rosa* but in fact normal practice of coercion by companies recruiting labor for private employers. We deal mainly with the first form in this section, with the second in the next. The structures of coercion at the work site, the compounds, are discussed in Chapter 5.

The recruitment and use of forced labor were governed by a bewildering array of legislative enactments whose nuances varied greatly over time and between British, French, Belgian and Portuguese areas. But the general political–economic circumstances in each area provide a guide to actual practices. Where industries lacked the capital to pay wages competitive with those offered by employers in neighboring territories, where ties between industry and the colonial state were strong, and where African labor supply fell short because of strong peasant production, compulsion tended to be used. Portuguese territories such as Mozambique made widespread use of forced labor for both public and private purposes, since Portuguese capitalists were undercapitalized by comparison to the British in neighboring South Africa and could not retain labor in any other way; a similar reason can be cited for the persistence of slavery among European employers in Portuguese areas. British administrators tended to be more averse to the collaboration of state and private interests than were the French, Belgians or Portuguese. Whereas in British areas formal government assistance in recruitment for private employers tended to be phased out quite early, in a case such as that of the Belgian Congo (now Zaire) the state retained a direct interest in the fortunes of the Katangan mines and continued to operate a state bureau of forced labor recruitment. In general, direct force tended to be used in the early stages of labor recruitment before the indirect but powerful effects of taxation, population pressure and agricultural underdevelopment had taken hold. Railway construction, for example, was often one of the earliest colonial development projects, and one on which forced labor was widely used.

The first demands for forced labor from Africans generally occurred in the context of military conquest. Faced with superior European firepower, or the threat of it, African societies had the choice either of resisting the British, French, Portuguese or Germans, of attempting to evade them or of actively allying with them. Given the prevalence of inter-group warfare, alliance was seen by some as an attractive option; but, given the heavy demands of the Europeans for food and for 'tribute labor' for porterage, road and railway work and troops, the price of submission could be high. In the end, whether through alliance or through conquest, large amounts of 'tribute labor' were exacted, none of which can be seen as 'voluntary' in the free market sense. Rather, force was usually applied either by the Europeans or by the chiefs and elders themselves to get their 'young men', clients or slaves to turn out to work.[2]

In a few cases warriors from groups that chose to ally with the Europeans fought enthusiastically on their side; Maasai 'levies', for example, helped the British pacify neighboring groups in Kenya between 1893 and 1900. They were paid handsomely in cattle, sheep and goats. However, this was still not wage labor, paid according to a precise calculation of labor time expended, goods produced or services rendered, but rather a sort of entrepreneurial partnership in which both sides shared the risks and rewards. The 1901 attempt by the British to transform the irregular Maasai levies into a permanent company of soldiers met with complete failure. Few warriors were interested in a long-term commitment away from home, even if they were well paid.[3] Many other Africans, however, in both British and French Africa, did join the colonial army as paid soldiers.

After conquest every colony instituted some system of forced labor. In British territories the practice varied greatly. The settler and mining areas of eastern, central and southern Africa all had early periods when official recruitment for both public and private employers took place, followed in central and southern areas by the establishment of powerful though non-governmental recruiting agencies. In the West African colonies and in Uganda, African peasant production was encouraged and the use of the forced labor was accordingly more restricted.

Significant exceptions to this picture can be found, however. In the northern territories of Ghana practicality triumphed over official scruples, and forced recruitment for the privately owned Tarkwa–Prestea gold-mines was allowed as part of government recruiting between 1906 and the 1920s. These mines, being small, had no recruiting system of their own and therefore depended on government assistance. They experienced labor shortages particularly for underground work, which was dangerous and unpleasant; worker confidence in the mines was heavily undermined by high death-rates in the mines from disease and accidents, rates in the order of 3–7% *per annum* in 1923, as compared to 1% *per annum* in the South African goldmines. Thus forced labor remained necessary to keep the mines open, and rates of desertion were high among recruits. High death-rates from accidents and pulmonary diseases such as tuberculosis apparently resulted not only from the appalling conditions in the mines, but also from the system of forced labor itself. Chiefs were said to be so lacking in authority that most of the able-bodied young men left for voluntary work on their own, leaving the chiefs to round up only the sick, the weak and those who could not defend themselves.[4]

In northern Nigeria it was not necessarily practicality so much as British devotion to indirect rule that dictated forced labor. There is a great contrast between the system of free wage labor and contractors, which was successfully used to build the Lagos railway at the turn of the century in the southern part of Nigeria, and the northern system of 'political' or forced labor. It was the obligation of the princes, or emirs, along the line to supply the labor, which was to be paid very low wages. The job of forcing men out of the villages to work ultimately fell to local district heads, who often rewarded themselves by extorting money from the laborers. Although workers had to remain on the job for only three to four weeks, one Bishop reported that conditions were akin to slavery: '... the men worked for nine or ten hours a day under revolting conditions, sometimes carrying heavy rails through deep mud without a break... if a man slacks or slips he is most cruelly beaten by those who are his overseers. Whilst if a man escapes from Baro and runs to his village, he is sent back by his overlord possibly after further beating.'[5]

In the French colonial territories there were at least three distinct forms of forced labor: the *indigénât*, or prison labor, the *préstations*, or annual tax in labor days, and the 'second portion' of the conscripted standing army. The labor tax, in particular, fell on every adult able-bodied male, who was required to provide from six to twelve days a year for local building projects: roads, bridges, telegraph lines, buildings, cotton shelters, dams, wells and landing-strips. In practice, those with the means could substitute a cash payment, while poorer Africans felt the greater burden. An intensive study of one administrative district, Koudougou in Upper Volta, home of the Mossi and Gourounsi groups, estimates that some five million person-days of free labor were extracted from Koudougou between 1917 and 1938.[6] In general, the system was so inefficient and unpopular that it prompted many migrations of voluntary workers into neighboring British territories, and it was largely phased out by the 1930s, though not officially abolished until 1946.[7]

The French had maintained a volunteer standing army, called the Senegalese Rifles, in French West Africa before World War I. During the War the units were transformed into a conscript army, and after the War conscription continued, in contrast to the demobilization in British colonies. Of those called up, some were placed on active duty and others into reserve units, which by the late 1920s began to be formed into labor brigades to serve for two to three years on public works. Their use was evidently widespread, especially on the Port of Dakar, on the Dakar–Niger railway, and on the construction of dams associated with the Office du Niger irrigation scheme in Soudan (Mali). Placed under control of private companies and working under deplorable conditions, Africans found service in the second portion in Mali so arduous and death-rates so high that many began to request entry into regular army service instead. Flight from military recruiters, desertion from the labor pool, outright refusal to serve even in the face of prison terms, and actual strikes over mistreatment were common forms of resistance by workers in the second portion.[8]

The extensive use of forced labor in Mozambique exemplifies the situation in Portuguese colonies. Here the system was imposed not only because of conditions within the colony, but also because of the vast flow of Mozambicans to the mines, cities and farms of Natal, Cape Colony and the Transvaal. The colonial economy of Mozambique was quite undeveloped in comparison to that of South Africa; wages were always much higher across the border, and despite the long journey and often hazardous mine work Mozambicans preferred to migrate. Only through force could the Portuguese retain labor at a price they could afford. In addition, the state wished to do everything it could to attract private capital, including the provision of forced labor. Labor was particularly critical in the port and capital city, Lorenço Marques, where most city services were run on contract by Portuguese or foreign firms. All these firms received generous contingents of forced labor, though Portuguese-owned ones could generally afford to pay less than British-owned ones and therefore relied more on such labor.[9]

The system was called *shibalo*, or slavery, by those subject to it. Every adult African male was liable for six months *shibalo* labor at a minimal wage, unless he could prove that he was voluntarily employed for wages full-time. In 1950 only about 7% of the available labor force could qualify for exemption on the basis of being a registered large-scale agriculturalist or cattle-raiser. As Marvin Harris has put it, the procurement of labor in rural areas 'early assumed the character of a hunt carried out at night in the hope of surprising the males who were at home before they had a chance to flee to the safety of one of the ubiquitous stations of the WNLA [the South African recruiting agency]. This hunt was conducted by agents of the native chiefs and sub-chiefs ...'[10] In the towns such as Lorenço Marques, 'when the Portuguese had a job they arranged a *rusga* – a round-up – the day before, and all Africans whose employers did not come to the police station to pick them up would be considered vagrants, and as such, volunteers for the job'.[11]

The Mozambique case graphically illustrates a general relationship between forced and voluntary wage-earning that has already been observed in the cases of northern Ghana and French West Africa, and was also evident in Kenya during war-time conscription,[12] namely that extensive use of forced labor tended to increase the supply of voluntary labor. The oppressive conditions of *shibalo* in Mozambique constituted a strong incentive for Tsonga and other Africans to leave for South Africa or southern Rhodesia in large numbers, as well as a disincentive to engage in traditional or peasant agriculture, since by doing so one became liable for forced labor. Where forced recruitment was applied in towns on a large scale, as in Lorenço Marques in the 1880s, it frightened off voluntary workers, making the town, in a vicious circle, even more dependent on forced labor.[13] Where forced and voluntary labor were used on the same work sites, the forced labor was often used on particularly difficult jobs that the voluntary workers refused to do, and was also often brought in to undercut strikes and labor protests by voluntary workers.

Forced labor everywhere met with some resistance. As with recruited contract labor, discussed below, the chief response of Africans was desertion, or escape. A number of circumstances could increase the likelihood that resistance and escape rates would be high. One such context was where the peasantry was prosperous and had very little interest in the income from wages, forced or not. This was the case around the tin-mines in northern Nigeria, where an experiment with forced labor was undertaken in 1918. Of 2,167 laborers from Bauchi Province, 885 deserted. There had been no guards, and desertions were unpunished, but application of the sanction of withholding pay until work was finished only produced increased desertions. Still, forced labor continued to be used on railway construction and porterage in the Plateau region.[14]

Harsh treatment, poor food, epidemics of contagious diseases, and unexpectedly heavy workloads were among the most widespread and tangible causes of desertions. The earliest recruits for the Tarkwa–Prestea gold-mines in Ghana deserted *en masse*: 540 were in the original party, but by the time they reached the mines after a lengthy journey, only 258 were left; a few months later a further 231 had deserted, and finally the remaining 27 left. An official who interviewed some of the runaways reported that at least six had been flogged, but that the main causes of desertion were 'the rains, the food which differed from their usual food ... and that they were frightened by the death of some of their party from pneumonia'. Another group from this same area had not been told that they would have to work underground, and upon arrival had refused to do so, many running off.[15]

The degree of chiefly control over workmen was another determinant of whether or not they rebelled. Michael Mason has pointed to the contrast, along the Baro–Kano railway line in northern Nigeria, between the Nupe workers, who did not desert or resist, and the neighboring Gwari, who did. Among the Nupe the structure of coercion was well grounded in traditional relationships between emirs and commoners. Backed by the colonial apparatus, the emirs turned out and controlled the forced labor, sometimes even exacting tribute from them of up to two-thirds of their meager wages. One prince, the Emir of Lapai, even moved from his capital to a camp near the railway line in order to exert greater control. Among the Gwari, however, political structures were much less hierarchical, and chiefly authority was more localized. In addition the colonial administration was more recently imposed and was short of manpower. Desertion rates were high among the Gwari, as were resistance to recruitment and to tax payment. One village, Gussoro, rebelled against a chief who had attempted to impose forced labor, killing a British political officer and eleven African policemen. These resistances tended to be timed at the beginning of the rainy season, when men needed to plant their own crops rather than work.[16]

LABOR RECRUITMENT

By the 1880s in South Africa, the Kimberley diamond-mines were in full production and the gold of the Witwatersrand was being opened up. The formal partition of the rest of the continent between the several European powers took place at the Conference of Berlin in 1886. The rich Katanga deposits of copper, and some tin and gold, went to Belgium; these began to be developed under an arrangement between the Belgian state and British capital between 1891 and 1911, with heavy direct investment by the Belgian state. Concurrently, the Southern Rhodesian (Zimbabwe) gold-fields were developed between 1903 and 1911 though the Northern Rhodesian (Zambian) copper-mines were not opened until 1926.

These were the massive mining developments that strained and then broke the limits of the voluntary labor supply in central and southern Africa.[17] The excess of demand over supply led to upward pressure on wages. Employer and government response in these territories was the formation of centralized recruiting agencies which were granted a monopsony over labor supplies in the territory. Mining interests in West and East Africa, such as the

Ghanaian gold-mines and the Nigerian tin-mines, also pushed for such monopsonistic recruiting systems, along with longer-term contracts and penal sanctions for contract breakers. But the mines in these areas never attained the dominance in the colonial economy that those in central and southern Africa did, and even if they could afford to mount such systems, colonial regimes usually vetoed them.

The Witwatersrand Native Labour Association (WNLA) was formed in 1900 by the South African Chamber of Mines; the Rhodesian Native Labour Bureau (RNLB) in 1903, and the Bourse du Travail du Katanga (BTK) in 1910; in the first two cases earlier versions of the agencies had operated for the preceding few years. The Northern Rhodesia Native Labour Association (NLA) was formed in 1929. In practice these agencies were never able to enforce a complete monopsony in the territory in question, and they operated in conjunction with smaller labor contracting firms which usually offered somewhat better terms to the worker when demand was high, and which sometimes specialized in recruiting more highly skilled workers.

The first function of these recruiting agencies was to create new supplies of labor or, failing this, to divert some of the supply being created by economic pressures from the high-wage markets to the low-wage ones. The second function was to achieve the supply goals without any increase, and preferably with a decrease, in African wages.[18] The agencies were substantially successful in these aims, contributing to long-term savings in total labor costs for the mines and more than offsetting the costs of the recruiting systems themselves.

The establishment of WNLA, for example, was accompanied by an agreement to reduce African wages from an average of R5 to R3 per month. The Chamber of Mines had been actively recruiting since 1896 and in 1900 approached the government of the Transvaal with a request that recruit-

Entering and leaving the work force

ing be a state enterprise. But the proposal was turned down, so WNLA was formed. Between 1890 and 1899 the black labor force on the mines rose from 14,000 to 99,000, while black wages actually fell.[19]

In Southern Rhodesia, the establishment of the RNLB made possible immediate wage reductions in 1904 and 1905, and again in 1906 and 1908, while still maintaining supply, whereas before that time there had been consistent upward pressure on wages.[20] Between 1906 and 1911 the RNLB supplied on average 13,000 laborers annually to Rhodesian employers, about 88% of them going to the mining industry, accounting on average for over 36% of the industry's requirements.[21] In Katanga, while the numbers recruited by the BTK increased five times between 1911 and 1915, basic wages for black miners fell, although total labor costs, which included compound construction, transport and food, rose.[22] Between 1916 and 1921, the number of workers recruited by the Bourse rose from 5,258 to 8,558, and the mean length of engagement rose from 5.7 months to 13.9, while the average wage costs to BTK employers actually declined, enabling them to hold total labor costs relatively steady, even while commodity prices, for example of food purchased by both miners and employers, were rising. Between 1919 and 1921 the declining value of the franc against the pound meant that the real value of wages for Congolese and Angolan workers was falling for an additional reason, since prices of the commodities they purchased were fixed in sterling.[23]

The fact that the recruiting agencies did not supply all the labor to the mines created a distinction between 'recruited' and 'voluntary' labor (though the latter category included many men recruited by smaller independent labor contractors). Charles Perrings has called attention to the importance of this distinction between the 'controlled' and the 'fringe' markets for labor in explaining worker behaviour and attitudes. The existence of more or less forcibly recruited labor had an effect both on the supply of voluntary labor – increasing it, as we noted earlier – and on wage differentials in the work force. The wage effect depended on the success of the official recruiting agency in meeting the demand. Where, as in Southern Rhodesia, the agency could produce an assured low-wage supply, this could enable employers to lower the wages of the remaining voluntary workers, since they were now to a certain extent expendable. But where, as in Katanga between 1911 and 1926, the demand soared far beyond what the Bourse could provide, wages in the fringe markets supplied by small contractors rose, leading to a widening differential between recruited and voluntary labor. The rise further undercut the ability of the Bourse to recruit, and provided great incentive for desertions.[24]

A third major function of the central recruiting agencies was to eliminate the competition among employers that was driving up wages; this factor operated both within the territory in question and on a regional basis. Within South Africa, for example, WNLA was formed specifically with this aim in mind, but it did not immediately succeed in eliminating the fierce competition between mining companies. It did achieve a negotiated monopsony in Mozambique, and it came to specialize in areas outside South Africa, while an analogous agency, the Native Recruiting Corporation, was organized in 1910 to recruit within the country. It took until 1919 for these agencies to achieve control over intercompany competition for labor.

Similarly, within Southern Rhodesia a main function of the RNLB was to channel labor to mines and other employers who, because of poor conditions and exploitative practices, could not secure independent labor.[25] In Katanga, competition for labor between railway construction and mining development was behind the decision to form the

BTK.[26] Thus, insofar as they were successful, the agencies served to protect exploitative employers and to remove an element of choice for workers in the marketplace.

Even more critical was the territorial competition for labor, in which the high-wage areas, mainly in South Africa, drew labor away from the low-wage areas. The function of the recruiting agencies, and of government forced labor systems, was to ensure that the peripheral territories got 'their' share of the supply. The whole of central and southern Africa can thus be looked upon as a single labor market divided into more central and more peripheral areas. Workers' ability to manipulate this market through independent geographical mobility was precisely what the recruiting agencies were attempting to control.

As the Rhodesian gold mines developed they had to compete for labor with South Africa until the formation of the RNLB. As Charles van Onselen put it, 'The loss of labour to the Transvaal and the activities of W.N.L.A. were a constant irritant to the industry and the B.S.A. Company alike, who felt justified themselves in drawing on the labour supplies from territories further north but resented Africans within the areas under their jurisdiction continuing to move to better labour markets in the south.' Pass laws were instituted and police and Native Commissioners patrolled the border along the Limpopo River. Still, many workers got through. Still another problem for employers was the passage of WNLA workers through transit compounds in Rhodesia. These groups bound for the Rand showed 'exuberant spirits', a description that could hardly be applied to the RNLB workers. An official inquiry in 1906 concluded that the practice was 'calculated to spread discontent among the natives ...'[27]

Before the mid-1920s WNLA, RNLB, the Katanga mines and the Lupa gold-fields of Tanzania all competed for the rich supplies of labor from Northern Rhodesia (Zambia).

The BTK recruited only within Katanga itself; the more outlying sources were the concessions of Robert Williams and Company (RWC), a British recruiting firm. Over half of the Union Minière de Haut Katanga's labor force came from outside the colony in the 1913–22 period, the majority being from north-eastern Rhodesia, the home of the Lunda, Chisinga, Mambwe, Iwa, Bemba, Bisa, Lala and Ngoni peoples.[28] With the exception of the Luapula – Mweru area, which was fertile and supplied food crops, fish, small livestock *and* much labor to the Katanga mines, most of the north-eastern Rhodesia plateau was both ecologically unsuited to the production of a significant agricultural surplus with the techniques then in use, and isolated from the main produce markets. Thus it supplied a great amount of voluntary labor, much of it channeled to Katanga through RWC. Katanga also drew smaller numbers of men from Nyasaland – an independent, non-recruited supply – northern Mozambique, Barotseland (in Zambia) and Angola. By the 1930s, as a result of taxation, coercive pressures and more organized administration, Katanga was drawing more heavily on its local supplies.[29]

In 1913 South Africa prohibited recruiting from all areas north of the 22°s latitude because of the very high death-rate from pneumonia of such 'tropical' workers in the southern mines. This move left part of northern Mozambique and Angola open for Katanga recruitment and reduced the pressure on Northern and Southern Rhodesia. By the end of the 1930s, with better medical knowledge and mine conditions, the WNLA again began recruiting in the north. At that time it was agreed that Southern Rhodesia and part of Mozambique were to be officially closed to the WNLA. But recruiting did take place in Malawi, Zambia, Botswana and Namibia, and drew from Angola and Tanzania from stations near the borders, according to quotas negotiated with each government. By 1952, of the 31,000 'tropicals' employed in the South African mines, about 23% came from Malawi, 16% from Tanzania, 10% from Namibia and 6% from Barotseland in Zambia, the remaining 45% presumably coming from Angola, northern Mozambique and Botswana.[30]

With the development of the copper-mines in Zambia, that territory began to take steps to claim some of this labor for itself. The higher wages prevailing elsewhere in the 1920s, particularly the dramatic upgrading of conditions in Katanga, made supply difficult and put the familiar upward pressure on wages. The Zambian mines established a joint recruiting agency in 1929, the Native Labour Association (NLA), and employed a former commandant of the Northern Rhodesian police as head. Like the BTK and the RNLB it offered fixed contracts and transport to and from the mines; unlike the other agencies it supplied skilled labor as well as unskilled. It operated both inside and outside Zambia, recruiting workers from Nyasaland, southern Mozambique *via* Rhodesia, and Angola *via* Barotseland. In 1930 the agency supplied over 10,000 men to the mines.[31] However, citing the still uncertain future of the industry, the Northern Rhodesian government refused to grant the NLA exclusive control over the internal supply, and continued to allow the RNLB and RWC recruiting concessions up to certain quotas.

In the regional competition for labor, the recruiting agencies tried on the one hand to negotiate official concession rights and quotas, and on the other hand to make good the concession, signing up workers by whatever method worked. The fact that the wage offered was higher in South Africa usually gave the WNLA an edge over competitors, even though the twelve-month contract was longer than that offered by some other agencies. But factors other than the wage were also variable – contract lengths, size of advances, deferred pay conditions – and different arrangements could appeal to different types of workers, depending on their situation in the rural economy.

The final and very critical function of labor recruitment systems was to serve as an effective method of control over African workers. In particular they frustrated the mobility of workers in the labor market, the very mobility which was the chief strategy open to migrant workers for defending themselves. The agencies achieved this goal largely through coercion and deception.

Throughout most of central Africa both recruited and forced labor systems came to be known as *chibaro* (*isibalo, shibalo, shibaru*), meaning slavery. From Natal and Mozambique to Nyasaland, Katanga and Rhodesia, Africans referred to all forced and recruited workers as 'slaves'.[32] A glance at recruitment methods and conditions will show why.

In many areas there was close cooperation between state agents and recruiters. In some districts of north-western Rhodesia between 1904 and 1910, local police simply rounded up people and handed them over to the RNLB. Those who refused to go were in some cases flogged and in others had their grain-stores burned down.[33] In Katanga after 1911 tax defaulters were routinely handed over to the BTK. In this area it was also widely but erroneously believed that voluntary, non-recruited work on the mines was forbidden.[34] In Mozambique, 'legally' recruited forced labor was sometimes turned over 'illegally' to RNLB agents at the border – for a commission.[35]

If government coercion was not available, as in less closely administered districts, recruiters were known to use direct force themselves, rounding up workers, rounding up women to await replacement by the men, or flogging escapees to serve as an example. Often, in such cases, they posed as government agents.[36] Often, they misled workers as to the length of their contract or where they were to be employed. In at least one case in Katanga, RWC transported workers to the mine by a very roundabout route so that they would not know how to return home.[37] It is impossible to estimate with any exactitude how widespread such practices were, but few researchers doubt that their frequency was great.

On the one hand these practices were used in rural areas to generate a labor supply that would not have existed otherwise. The widespread rates of desertion back to rural areas indicate as much. On the other hand, the same methods of force and trickery were used to divert a part of the high-wage, voluntary flow of workers into the low-wage jobs. In this case the recruiting agency simply waited for taxation and economic forces to push people off the land and then skimmed off a percentage of the labor at critical points in the migration routes. One pretext was provided by the sleeping sickness scare. In north-eastern Rhodesia in 1910 the RNLB took advantage of this situation to acquire exclusive recruiting rights on the grounds that it alone, rather than the Katangan agencies, could ensure adequate medical inspection. In practice all workers attempting to migrate voluntarily were caught and sent for a compulsory examination by the Bureau's doctors. In the words of one contemporary, 'All the boys required to do was to engage with the Bureau, and if they did that, that was sufficient to get rid of the suspicion of having sleeping sickness.'[38]

More characteristic perhaps was the stationing of RNLB agents at catch-points along migration routes; ideal for this purpose were the ferries in Rhodesia, which crossed rivers flowing east while workers attempted to travel south. In 1908 the government put RNLB in sole charge of 'free ferries', which they used as a lure to obtain thousands of formerly independent workers. Many such workers became afraid to travel along the main routes for fear of being intercepted by the Bureau. Migration became a hazardous game of hide-and-seek with the agents.[39]

There was a limit to how long trickery, fraud and the

gross misrepresentation of terms of employment could be put over on Africans in any given district. Such methods could only be used for short periods, often in areas new to the labor market, where African market intelligence had yet to develop. But workers who experienced at first hand the hazards and limited rewards of recruitment soon returned to spread the bad word. Van Onselen points out that the RNLB had to move continually from district to district as gullibility was exhausted, as in 'some primitive rural robber-economy'. The number of different areas the Bureau operated in between 1903 and 1910 was quite remarkable considering that it only supplied some 10,000 workers annually.[40]

Wherever possible, the more experienced African workers attempted to avoid recruitment agencies. For example, by the 1920s in Zambia workers had become highly dependent on wage labor and strongly preferred to find their own way to the Copperbelt and to apply for work under the particular boss or department which appealed to them. Many preferred to work for contractors because of the looser system of control at work and in the compounds. Thus, two-thirds of the Copperbelt labor was voluntary in the 1920s.[41] And in 1936–7, after active recruiting for Katanga was ended in Zambia, over 10,000 workers went across the border to work in the Belgian mines, exclusively on a voluntary basis.[42] In the settler colony of Kenya, recruiting agencies were active through the 1920s, particularly in getting workers from Nyanza Province, for sisal plantations and railway construction. But by the end of the 1920s more and more workers began avoiding the labor agents, and the increase in the voluntary supply made recruitment no longer necessary.[43] In South Africa, however, recruitment remained mandatory for all workers entering the country from outside.

Worker preferences sometimes forced recruiters to

modify their terms if they wished to get laborers; by 1913 the BTK in Katanga, for instance, had shortened the contract time demanded from recruits and was having greater success.[44] Or workers shifted from one recruiter to another, as in 1919 in Angola, where, only two years after the beginning of RWC engagements, large numbers were reported to be engaging with smaller labor contractors, who offered shorter contracts, higher cash wages and immediate as opposed to deferred pay.[45] Finally, recruiting agencies were usually dismal failures in areas very near to the work sites, both because of the greater sophistication of the potential workers, and because of the market for produce which opened up. Hence the difficulties of the RNLB in recruiting local Shona and Ndebele workers before 1912, and the difficulties of the BTK in developing Congolese supplies near to the mines.

Where the recruiting agency could not be avoided, African protest showed itself mainly through the characteristic tactic of desertion. In all areas outside South Africa, and even there to some extent, rates of 'breaking contract', to go either back to the rural economy or to a better job, were high. Punishment, however, was likely to be harsh, especially where the system was efficiently administered, as in Northern Rhodesia between 1919 and 1922, or in Angola between 1917 and 1921, where 47% of all deserters from RWC were traced and recaptured.[46] In some cases deserters would be flogged, or their home villages attacked. Other risks could be even greater, especially if the worker were weakened by sickness or lack of food. Untold numbers of Africans must have died in the bush while attempting to reach home after escaping from a recruiter.

The fact that recruiting agencies were relatively successful in some parts of central and southern Africa may be traced in part to force, but also to the fact that in order to walk the hundreds of miles between home and work sites, an African had already to possess a number of resources. He had to be in excellent health, to be able to provide himself with the necessary food and clothing for the journey, and to be free from immediate obligations at home. There were no bicycles, no animal transport, no motor vehicles and few railways. Workers from north-eastern Rhodesia, for example, faced on average a 750-mile walk to labor centers. Such journeys constituted a large 'up-front' investment of time and resources before wage-earning even began. A great many Africans could not afford such an investment; it was often their very poverty that drove them to seek work. At this point the labor agent stepped in, offering blankets, food, free transport, even advances on wages to meet immediate family needs. The worker in fact paid for these services through his acceptance of the lowest wages, longest contracts and worst working conditions in the area, and often, in addition, he started work under a burden of indebtedness. But it was not his gullibility that made him accept such terms, rather it was his poverty. The labor recruiting system throve on the exploitation of poverty. In Mozambique, for example, 1918 was a year of drought, and the RNLB agent reported that the peasants were only agreeing to contracts because they were starving. He added that 'as the Gangs get their issues of blankets, money and food on leaving Tete there are numbers of their friends and relations from their homes waiting for them to give them practically the whole of what they had received'. Clearly, the advances given were an important factor in getting them to sign on.[47]

Most writers have been too quick to assume that systems of advance payments always worked to the disadvantage of Africans. If the advances were large enough, they might be a short-term disadvantage to the individual worker but of immediate advantage to the worker's household and to the wider rural social system. Workers' family heads and rural chiefs sometimes had an interest in maintaining the advance system, or deferred payment systems, which assured them of an income and also tended to ensure that the migrant would return home and that his money would benefit the rural household rather than being spent on jewelry, liquor, clothes, prostitutes and the other town temptations that migrants found so difficult to resist.

William Beinart has argued convincingly that such was the case for the Mpondo at the turn of the century in the Transkei.[48] Even though the option of non-contracted labor was quite well known, and used in neighboring areas, some 80% of migrants from Pondoland chose to go through labor agents in 1908. They did so in order to get an advance, in at least half of the cases an advance in the form of one or two cattle. It is true that middlemen – the local traders who made the advances – had a stake in the system and made enormous profits from it. But the evidence suggests that the Mpondo themselves were in favor of the system even though the wage they received was lower than they could have earned independently and the cattle price overvalued. Why?

It was not simply that there was a situation of immediate emergency in Pondoland, although Mpondo labor migration and the cattle-advance system both seem to have had their origins in the destruction of herds by rinderpest in 1897 and the consequent pressing need to rebuild. It was also that cattle in particular were the best investment possible in the rural economy at that time: they were a major source of food; they constituted bridewealth, making it possible for a young man to marry; and oxen were increasingly important in cultivation. Livestock were exchangeable for other goods, or could be sold for cash; and, most important, they reproduced quickly. As Beinart puts it,

In the circumstances, placing an advance beast in the kraal before the migrant left home was far more sensible than waiting, perhaps for a year, for the migrant to return home with cash and buy an animal. A cow in the kraal could make the difference between having a little milk and having none; an ox, the difference between being able to make up a span, or help a neighbour to do so, and having to dig the fields with hoes. A year was a long time to live without these resources. Most important of all, a cow could drop a calf in the period of the worker's absence and the advance would be doubled.[49]

Events suggest that in these years cattle were a productive investment, for in the first decade of the twentieth century the Mpondo extended cultivation with ox-drawn ploughs and increased their export of crops, as described in Chapter 2 above.

Systems such as cattle advances illustrate the struggle of African peasant societies against the immediate and complete dominance of capital. In this case a system emerged out of the interaction of capitalist intermediaries and Africans, and reflected the interests of both *versus* those of employers. In addition, the persistence of the system both attests and contributed to the strength and resilience of the rural household and its control over its members. Even after the system was abolished, many young men accepted instead a new system of deferred pay which continued to give some protection to the rural family. Here we see the demands of the rural economy and household governing choices Africans made about the terms on which they would enter the wage economy.

However, the advances given in this case were so large as to be a far different proposition from a blanket or two or free transport. Sometimes a worker could complete the whole of his one- or two-year contract on the mines without ever seeing anything more than the monthly ten shillings in cash made mandatory by the state, the total wage having been paid to the trader as compensation for cattle advanced. The advance was so large that the incentive to desert before contract completion was considerable. It was difficult to trace the animal advanced when this happened, since it could be hidden or sold, or could easily have died. A dead animal was another strong incentive for the worker to desert, since the trader was not bound to replace the animal. The high level of desertions, pass forgeries, contract complaints and legal battles arising out of the cattle-advance system led to the state – under pressure from WNLA, whose losses were great, and the mining industry – to abolish the system as soon as its initial function of attracting hitherto unwilling Mpondo into the labor market was deemed to have been accomplished. By 1910 it was declared illegal, along with all other advances over £5 in whatever form. But such was the appeal of the cattle advances that they persisted illegally into the 1920s. Capital was ultimately triumphant, but not without a struggle.

Aside from advances, the paramount issues for workers who *opted* for the recruitment systems were likely to be seasonal time of recruitment and length of contract, since those involved tended to be workers who were attempting to juggle wage work and agriculture. Africans living near the mines in Katanga and Zambia were successful for some years in enforcing the agricultural cycle; in 1916 the labor supplies produced by both the BTK and RWC showed declines during the wet, or growing, season from November to March. From 1916 to the early 1920s, six-month contracts, repatriation and deferred pay (which protected workers against the decline of the franc against the pound) were popular among Zambian workers going to Katanga. And in 1924 the BTK's recruiting difficulties in western Lulua were caused by competition from an independent firm, Correa Brothers, which engaged men on six-month contracts which were much more easily integrated into the agricultural cycle than the 14 months of BTK engagements.[50] By contrast, the principal issue for non-recruited workers was wages, since they tended to be more dependent on wage-earning. When these workers deserted, it tended to be a move aimed at getting a better job, taking advantage of regional wage differentials, rather than a move back to the rural economy.[51]

The institution of recruiting systems forcibly and often brutally created wage labor. The systems also kept wages low, and limited African maneuverability, and therefore advancement, in the labor market. In so doing, they also probably delayed the inevitable disintegrating effects of full wage labor on traditional society. Viewed in historical perspective, this poignant combination of negative and positive effects makes it difficult to arrive at a wholesale condemnation of all such systems, especially where rural economies were vital and functioning.

In most parts of Africa today, recruiting systems are no longer operative, having been succeeded by a large enough 'voluntary' supply. They persist, however, in South Africa, where they are an integral part of the structure of apartheid. All employed workers, whether from inside South Africa or outside, must arrive through labor bureau channels and are subject to contracts of fixed length, compulsory repatriation and other labor controls. In most parts of South Africa, rural agricultural options are few or non-existent, negating any argument that the worker's family or community might benefit from constraints on his or her labor-market participation. It is in this context that some of the largest protests against recruitment systems have taken place.

'Desertion' has often been used as a collective, rather than simply an individual, form of protest, but in at least one southern African case desertion took on the proportions of a massive strike against the contract system. This was the strike by the Ovambo in Namibia in 1971–2. The Ovambo have become increasingly dependent on wage labor, and the development of crop production for sale has been slow because of official trade restrictions, lack of transport and ecological conditions. Over the past twenty years, food shortages have become a major factor behind labor migration.[52]

For the last fifty years the recruitment and distribution of labor from this area have been mainly the monopoly of SWANLA, the South West Africa Native Labour Association, administered by the major Namibia employers. All workers must go through a recruiting agency; there is hardly any possibility of independent migration. The standard minimum contract of at least one year has vitiated any attempt by migrants to combine periods of absence with the agricultural cycle. The recruiting organization determines wages, length of service and employer. As in South Africa, pass laws make it difficult to desert or break contract, and on termination of a contract repatriation is now compulsory, Labor is allocated to the major white-owned industries of farming, fishing, mining and commerce, all of which employ exclusively contract labor, skilled and unskilled. Compulsory residence in closed, barracks-like bachelor compounds, together with ethnic homogeneity, has intensified Ovambo worker consciousness on the job.

Although collective strike action has been undertaken periodically at the point of production, it has been highly vulnerable to state repression and has not been notably successful. For this reason, the tactic of mass withdrawal from the contract system may have seemed more likely to work.

Another key factor in the years preceding the strike was the rising political consciousness in Namibia and the consequent formation in 1960 of the South West Africa People's Organization (SWAPO), a national anti-colonial movement. Contract workers have been the organization's most consistent and militant basis. The year 1971 marked an escalation of anti-colonial political activity in Namibia, spurred by the ruling of the World Court that South Africa's continued occupation of the territory was illegal.

The strike was part of a calculated political campaign, supported by SWAPO, to end the contract-labor system. It was also the occasion of a spontaneous mass outburst of discontent. The strike call was spectacularly successful. By December 20, 1971, 11,500 workers were on strike. By mid-January, 13,500 had been transported by rail back to Ovamboland and some 21,000 had engaged in some kind of protest. The vast majority of Ovambo workers in towns and mines cooperated, as well as substantial numbers of farm and domestic workers.

The foundation of the workers' demands was the abolition of the SWANLA monopoly, its replacement by a free labor market, and the ending of pass laws. They protested against low wages and compulsory repatriation. They described the contract system as a form of slavery, because blacks were 'bought' by SWANLA and forced to live in 'jail-like' compounds.[53] These demands struck at the root of the apartheid system, and therefore would not be granted in full by the authorities. What the Ovambo did achieve were a few concessions, such as renewal of contracts with the same employer without having to return home, and wage increases. On the other hand, after the strike there was a great increase in what employers called 'desertion', and what the Ovambo viewed as their right to leave an unsatisfactory job and look for a better one. New and more stringent legal controls over desertion were imposed in subsequent months. On the whole, the contract system remained much as it had been before.

The Ovambo strike was unusual in its focus on abolishing the labor contract system, but it illustrates a tactical maneuver often used by striking migrant workers: withdrawal into the countryside. Strikers resolved not only to cease work, but to return to Ovamboland rather than remain in town, and to negotiate from there, refusing any new contracts until a settlement was reached. The strike committee admonished workers to 'raise as big a crop as possible, to make Ovambo independent of contract labour'.[54] But, as Richard Moorsom has pointed out, in this case there were two major contradictions to this strategy: first, that it coincided with the authorities' desire to avoid further unrest in 'white' areas, and, second, that in reality it was no longer economically possible for the Ovambo to opt out of wage labor indefinitely. The longer-term trend in South Africa and associated areas will probably be toward more direct confrontation with governmental authorities.

§ 5 §

MIGRANTS AT THE WORK PLACE

The second basic dimension which governs workers' attitudes and actions is the character of the work itself, the social and technical division of labor on the job. Included here are the technical and skill level of the work; the spatial arrangements and communication patterns among workers; the hierarchy of power, and the strategies and institutions of worker control; the levels and kinds of remuneration; the conditions of housing, health and nutrition. These factors are intrinsic to the work place, as opposed to those having to do with the labor market, which are largely extrinsic. They are a complex of material, ideological and power variables.

If avoidance of recruitment, desertion and 'communal' rebellion have been the chief forms of worker protest against the process of incorporation into the wage-labor force, other forms of resistance become appropriate at the work place itself. These may range from a) forms of psychological adjustment or escapism, such as absenteeism, drug and alcohol use, religious movements and formation of worker sub-cultures; to b) overt and covert tactics designed to increase worker control over the work process, for example collective bargaining over tasks and time, slowdowns, inefficiency and even sabotage; to c) tactics aimed at increasing wages and rewards, such as theft, unionization, and economistic strikes.[1] The tendencies toward the use of these different forms have varied according to differing skill levels, to degree of proletarianization, and to differing managerial control strategies.

For our purposes in this book, the central question that arises is whether uniformity of work place factors can overcome the frequent division in the African work force between fully and partly proletarianized workers, between those of differing labor market status.[2] That is, if there is a tendency among semi-proletarianized migrant workers to respond to oppressive work conditions through desertion or individualized solutions, under what circumstances is this tendency overcome; do migrants participate in collective on-site work actions such as trade unions and strikes? One difficulty in answering this question lies in the fact that the main work place divisions of skill and pay often *coincide* with the labor-market divisions. Frequently semi-proletarianized workers are given low-skilled, low-wage jobs, and in this way their labor-market situation can impede their upward mobility at the work place. We are also concerned, then, with the differences in labor action between skilled and less-skilled workers. We examine these questions for three different industrial categories of workers: miners, port and dock workers, and domestic workers. They work in industries where the organization of production and the strategies of managerial control are all quite different, but where the incidence of migrancy has been high.

The conditions of early industrialization in a peripheral area of the world-economy have determined the industrial structure of Africa's work force. Initially, investment was largely in the extractive industries of mining and agriculture, and in transport and communication networks. Miners, agricultural workers and railway and dock workers were numerous. So were domestic workers, since European settlers had a propensity to employ large numbers of them, and in some towns many commercial and construction workers were found. Factory workers, on the other hand, were a relatively small category except in South Africa, where local capital financed garment, textile and other industries in the 1920s and 1930s. After World War II, however, the number of factory workers in western, eastern and central Africa began to increase as international capital showed greater interest in locating processing facilities there. Aside from white-collar workers, who were among the earliest to form formal associations to press their interests, the most militant labor activity has historically come from dock workers, miners and railway workers.[3] But, in fact, the conditions and organization of work in each of these industries were quite different, and the militancy came about, or was inhibited, for quite different reasons.

DOCKWORKERS

Throughout most of the colonial era, the docking industry was run largely on the basis of daily-paid casual labor. The various tasks of the port — stevedoring (loading and unloading ships), shore-handling, and lighterage (the use of intermediate vessels, which were sometimes necessary) — were often the monopoly of a few private companies or of a consortium of companies including the government-owned railway administration. Because of the labor-intensive methods and the irregularity of ship arrivals, colonial employers had an interest in maintaining a large reserve of surplus labor in the city. Laborers congregated at the dock gates each morning; some were engaged, many were turned away except at periods of peak demand. In this way employers adjusted their payrolls daily and avoided the costs of a longer contract system.

The system provided little security of income to workers. Wages might seem high, but actual earnings depended on frequency of employment. A 1945 study in Mombasa determined that of some 7,200 Africans registered as port casual workers, about 3,000 actually worked less than 15 days a month.[4] In such a situation, those who had no alternative source of income, either in urban or rural areas, were very likely to become discontented. Those with another job, or with productive farms nearby, might, on the other hand, prefer the casual system.

Dock workers were among the least 'controlled' of African workers in the 1920s, 1930s and 1940s. Since labor supply was always adequate because of high-sounding wages and the possibility of other employment in the port city, dock workers were not usually quartered in closed compounds like miners. Employer paternalism was not widespread in the industry until after the decasualization of the docks in the 1950s. Although in South Africa the municipality and some private employers constructed barracks for workers, in East Africa the provision of housing was mainly left to the workers, and its necessarily poor quality became a further cause for discontent.

The lack of effective employer control, the uncertain wages, and the poor urban living conditions, must be put together with two other factors in explaining dockers' propensity to strike in these years: the spatial unity provided by the port itself, as a large industrial enterprise, and the strategic location of workers at points of communication. News could spread quickly from port to port *via* sailors and ship workers. Strike action at the port could be quickly followed by other workers throughout the city. The port was strategic too in its role in the colonial economy; port workers derived much of their power from their ability to shut down the entire colonial import–export operation by merely walking off the job. Technologically, employers had as yet no alternative to relying on large numbers of semi-skilled stevedores and shore-handlers. The digging of deep-water berths reduced the lighterage work of moving goods from large ships to small ones, and the installation of cranes reduced goods handling time, but it also created the skilled post of crane operator. The introduction of forklifts had a similar effect. Overall, the increasing volume of traffic in most ports strained their technical capacity, and container technology did not begin to be used until the 1970s.

Such was the background to the remarkable series of strikes that took place along the East African coast in the years surrounding World War II. The immediate precipitating factors were increased work-load and war-time inflation, which drove up prices but not wages. In Durban, there were dock strikes in 1941 and 1942, and riots and a general strike in 1949; in Mombasa there were strikes in 1934 and 1939, and a general strike in 1947; in Dar-es-Salaam there were strikes in 1939 and 1943, and a general strike in 1947; and in Zanzibar City and Lourenço Marques there were strikes in 1948.[5] In addition to this war-time cluster, there were important later strikes in the mid-1950s in Durban, Mombasa and Dar-es-Salaam, and earlier ones in the South African ports of Cape Town and East London, as well as Durban.[6]

The most significant aspect of nearly all these strikes was the important, and in some cases the initiating, role of the casual, unskilled, daily-paid workers. In 1939, in both Mombasa and Dar-es-Salaam, the casual workers, rather than the relatively few who were on monthly or 'permanent' terms, were the first to go on strike. In the general strikes of 1947 in both these cities, and in Zanzibar City in 1948, both the daily-paid and the monthly workers all went on strike, seemingly in concert. And in Durban all three of the strikes mentioned appeared to be led by the *togt*, or daily-paid workers, since there were only a very few, the employees of the railway administration, who were on weekly terms. Several of the strikes actually began in the *togt* barracks.

Hemson writes that the *togt* workers 'were probably the only group of black workers in Durban who provided leadership from among their own ranks without relying on non-laboring educated strata...'[7] Sometime in 1939, Zulu Phungula was elected their leader and was a key figure in succeeding strikes.

Several writers have suggested that this clustering of strikes along the East African coast was not unrelated, that action in one place served to spur unrest in others.[8] In any case the main issue in each of the general strikes was the same, the failure of wages to keep up with prices, and in each case the strike spread quickly from the port to the rest of the town. In Mombasa, the first all-workers organization in the colony emerged, the African Workers' Federation, led by a Mombasa clerk, Chege Kibachia, who spoke for workers during the strike. In Dar-es-Salaam, the Dockworkers' and Stevedores' Union was formed in 1947 directly out of the experience of the strike. In Durban, following the demise in the 1920s of the ICU (an organization rather similar to the Kenyan AWF), the daily-paid workers had turned to Phungula as their leader, but after his banishment worker organization was forced underground by harsh oppression by the South African state. Hemson argues that one of the key strategies of worker control, the barracks for *togt* workers, actually served the contrary purpose of keeping a bedrock of informal organization alive. Contrary to the argument advanced by van Onselen and others, that compounds are 'total institutions' which make worker collective action impossible, the evidence suggests that in this case the compounds facilitated greater communication among workers and more effective organization among these workers when on strike.[9]

The war-time upheavals among dock workers were a major factor in prompting the colonial state to transform the structure of dock labor. But the two areas, South Africa on the one hand and East Africa on the other, moved in fundamentally different directions in dealing with the crisis, their responses being reflected in the opposite fortunes of the migrant-labor systems in the two areas. South Africa moved toward institutionalizing migrancy through changing port labor from the daily-paid system to limited contracts and influx control, whereas Kenya, Tanzania and Zanzibar took the first steps toward stabilizing port labor in town, changing more workers from daily to monthly contracts.

It is tempting to ask – with the benefit of hindsight – whether dock workers were in some sense struggling to preserve and upgrade the casual and migrant systems, or whether they were in fact pressing for fuller proletarianization. Hemson tells us that in Durban in 1941, 'Phungula was arguing for the dock workers to be accepted as full proletarians ... and to be paid a wage which would enable workers and their families to live under urban conditions.' To a government threat that workers could 'go home' if they did not wish to accept a wage offer, Phungula countered: 'The government must show us where to go because our homes are here in Durban.'[10] Fred Cooper, on the other hand, has argued, for Mombasa, that the workers themselves were 'the great defenders of casual work' and that 'steady work had never been a demand of the dockworkers'.[11]

Cooper's contention is surely overstated for Kenya. It rests on the slim evidence of official prejudice, and fails to account for the leading role of up-country Kikuyu and Nyanza workers in all the major labor protests of the period; these workers were the very ones who, as long-distance migrants from land-squeezed rural economies, least wished to work on an uncertain, casual basis. But it may well be true that the local Mijikenda strongly preferred casual work, since they went to the rural areas frequently, though their economies could hardly be said to be flourishing. Differences in degree of proletarianization probably made for differences in worker outlook.[12] Mijikenda were, in fact, the ones most hurt by the decasualization regulations imposed in the early 1950s, under which those who did not work 15–20 shifts a month were deregistered, that is, not allowed to work at all. In general, however, there was very little direct protest against the decasualization scheme in Mombasa, because of the rise in incomes. Between 1947 and 1958, while the food-price index for Africans rose 147%, the wages of stevedoring casual labor rose 204% and those of shore-handling casual labor 255%.[13]

But in Durban the limited decasualization that was represented by the contract system was not coupled with any increase in wages and therefore meant an intensification of the amount of labor that had to be expended to achieve the same income. It encountered strong resistance. In 1959 workers were quoted as saying: 'The employers want to kill us with overtime. In the past we used to take off a day or two whenever we felt tired, but now that we are employed on a weekly basis we could not do this.' The weekly wage was Sh. 60, compared to a potential of Sh. 84 for a full week's work under the daily system.[14]

The conclusion most supported by the slender evidence as to dock workers' consciousness at this time is that they wanted an increase in their wages and standard of living without any intensification of their work burden. Any system other than daily-paid work would be evaluated according to whether it promised to achieve these ends. In Kenya decasualization meant an income increase for at least half of the workers, whereas in Durban the continuing low wages and the intensification of labor outweighed the limited increases in stability that were offered.

In sum, the work-place conditions of migrant dock workers in the 1940s – the uncertain incomes, the lack of employer control, the poor living conditions, the strategic position in the economy and in relation to other urban workers and to workers in other ports along the coast – all made it possible for migrants to become leading worker militants. In addition, there was, at this time, relatively little skill and income differentiation in the work force, and only a small number of non-migrant, educated or skilled workers. Migrants were in the majority, but this did not mean any lack of worker leadership; rather it promoted a consciousness of all-worker solidarity.

A very different picture can be found among the Lagos, Nigeria, dock workers today. Here, limited decasualization has divided the work force between a permanently employed, better-paid and well-unionized section working for the state-controlled Nigerian Ports Authority (NPA), and a daily-paid, less-skilled and little-unionized section working for private contractors. On the NPA staff about 75% are permanently employed and about 25% are engaged as daily-paid, temporary or casual workers; the contractors employ probably an equal number of workers, of whom at least 70% are daily-paid and unskilled. Peter Waterman has distinguished these two categories of worker as 'two separate universes of wage labor'. The relative privilege of the regularly employed NPA worker is evident in the fact that, even if we assume the casual dock worker to work a full month, he will still earn less than half the pay of an NPA manual worker. Yet official figures for registered dock labor in the 1960s show that between 47% and 70% of them worked for less than 15 days a month.[15]

The desultory history of unionism among the contractor, or dock worker, section, and its lack of success in raising wages, suggest that this group of workers is in a much weaker position than the NPA group. Even among the latter group, when the unions have occasionally tried to take up the grievances of the daily-paid staff, or to get them transferred to permanent terms, they have not been notably successful. In one case in 1963, when the NPA proposed to transfer all their daily-paid workers in Port Harcourt to private contractors, the NPA Workers' Union resisted, and attempted to negotiate at least some severance pay for them; but it was able only to delay the action for a few years. About 2,000 were ultimately dismissed, with no compensation whatsoever.[16] In 1963 there was a large strike of Lagos casual dock workers, which was a disastrous failure. Many workers and headmen lost their jobs, and contractors refused to grant wage increases. In the Nigerian general strike of June, 1964, dock workers again participated *en masse*, and the port was paralysed during this period. This time they did achieve a wage increase, although the nationally negotiated wage settlement initially applied only to the public sector, and it was necessary for the dockers to go on another ten-day strike in August in order to get their new rates. Waterman points out that, willing as the dockers were to strike, they were unable to beat the government and employers on their own in these strikes. It was only as part of a general strike, resulting in government pressure for a general wage increase throughout the country, that any success was achieved.[17] Migrant and casual workers were no longer in as strong a position as they had been during the colonial period in East Africa.

MINERS

If dockers were among the least controlled of colonial migrant workers, miners were among the most, because of the labor-repressive institution of the compound, still used in its more 'closed' form throughout South Africa, and in more relaxed and open forms in central Africa. Moreover, more than dock workers, mine workers are highly differentiated according to skill. For this reason, and because the mines draw from many different African societies, the work forces have usually combined migrant, less-proletarianized workers with longer-service, more-proletarianized workers, providing an opportunity to compare the roles of these two categories in industrial protest. However, during the colonial era in central Africa, and still today in South Africa, the top skill levels have been monopolized by white rather than black workers. This racial factor has had a solidifying effect on the black working class.

Whereas the docks in the colonial era usually had an over-supply of labor, the mines were faced with the problem of attracting and retaining a labor force in conditions fraught with danger to life and health. The primary function of the compound, an institution peculiar to Africa, is labor control. Its origins lie in the diamond-mines of Kimberley, South Africa, where owners faced an additional problem, particularly rife in that industry, of theft of the small, valuable diamonds for sale in the illicit diamond-buying trade.

By 1885 the compound at DeBeers' Consolidated Mines at Kimberley had developed into a quasi-military enclosure. It was a square, surrounded by a corrugated iron fence ten feet high, with a single gate as an entrance. Access to the mine-workings was through a covered way and an inclined shaft. When African workers entered the compound on two- or three-month contracts, they effectively lost all access to the outside world. They were searched each day after work, a process which involved humiliating invasions of personal privacy. And a few years later the entire compound came to be covered by fine wire mesh, designed to prevent parcels of diamonds being thrown over the fence.[18] The effectiveness of this system in controlling thefts and desertions cannot be doubted.

The DeBeers compound was the prototype of the 'closed compound' which also came to be used on the Rand for gold-miners, where it functioned solely as a labor control measure, having been introduced partly in response to the 1901–6 labor crisis: a shortage of labor, very high rates of desertion, and the need to expand production.[19] The system which came into existence in Southern Rhodesia was the slightly less coercive 'open compound,' while the compounds on the Northern Rhodesian copper-mines were more 'open' still. Like the Rand, the Southern Rhodesian gold-mines had an appalling health record and falling cash wages, and within the regional economy they were forced to compete with the more attractive labor markets in South Africa. Such factors argued for the compound system, but these mines actually had fewer problems getting labor than did the Rand, since they drew on a large local market and thousands of workers from further north. Nor did they compete with a local manufacturing industry for their labor supply. These factors made possible the somewhat more open compound, typically a three-tiered system in which the inner or square compounds housed short-term or recruited workers, those least proletarianized, most unskilled and lowest paid; the huts of single workers surrounding the inner compound housed longer-term workers, and these were separated from an outer area of huts of married workers with families, the group least likely to desert. The Rand, by contrast, used only the single male migrant; women and children were not allowed on the mines.[20] These patterns of compound layout are still in use today, with barracks-like accommodation of at least 12 men to a room, and often enforced tribal segregation.

Technologically, copper-mining required higher proportions of skilled and semi-skilled labor than did gold-mining, although this varied from mine to mine according to the nature of the ore deposits.[21] In addition, the later development of the Northern Rhodesian mines meant that they had to compete with South Africa, Southern Rhodesia and Katanga for labor. These factors pushed the Copperbelt mine-owners toward a policy of labor stabilization, with less reliance on the more repressive aspects of the compound. Married workers were encouraged by the provision of small plots to bring families. Welfare, nutrition, health and accident policies were somewhat more advanced. Still, a high fence surrounded the whole compound, which was like a small township, and carefully guarded gates monitored the flow of persons in and out. Only mine employees, their dependants and temporary registered guests were allowed in.[22]

In colonial Rhodesia and in South Africa, compounds were under the unchallengeable authority of a white Compound Manager, often a man with a military background. Indeed, military terminology was much in use, the quarters being referred to as 'barracks' and an African strike as a 'mutiny'. Discipline was harsh, and it was enforced by the compound police, who were armed, normally, with whips – the *chikote* in Rhodesia and the *sjambok* in South Africa. Police were often informers, informing management of a threatened strike or desertion. Police also roused the men for work in the morning, typically at 3 or 4 a.m. Failure to appear, or failure to complete a full day's work would result in the worker's 'ticket' not being signed, and loss of a day's pay. Any 'loafing', feigned illness, leaving of work for any reason, falling asleep on the job, or damage to mine equipment would result in punishment. Frequently, 'boss boys' or white supervisors would physically assault workers directly. Or they would report the offense to the Compound Manager, who imposed fines, jail terms or, very frequently, whippings. On two of the largest mines in Southern Rhodesia, jails had cells equipped with stocks, to which workers were tied while being cruelly whipped. In the not unusual cases where African workers died as a result of such brutalities, white juries invariably exonerated the mine personnel. Under such an oppressive regime, black workers were nearly powerless, and sometimes psychologically colonized, tending fatalistically to accept the system.[23]

In order to cope in such repressive 'closed' compounds, workers frequently develop a counter-culture, a 'Brotherhood' of group solidarity through which they struggle to retain their own definition of the situation. This workers' culture has been graphically depicted by Robert Gordon, from his experience as a Personnel Officer in a Namibian diamond-mine in 1974.[24] Like all mines in the colonial period, and like South African mines today, the labor force in the Namibian mine is divided into two caste-like strata based on race. By law, no black is allowed to be in a position of authority over a white. The Project Manager, who reports to the Head Office in South Africa, the Compound Manager, the Resident Engineers and the small number of skilled white artisans, all supervise gangs of blacks who do the actual labor. The only supervisory position for blacks is that of Boss Boy, who is in reality a go-between between black workers and white supervisors. The highest-paid black workers are clerks, policemen and drivers. The ratio of white to black wages is estimated to be about 14 to 1. All black workers are migrant contract workers, many of whom were part of the famous Ovambo strike of 1971–2 against the contract system.

Blacks are well aware not only of the oppressive and unequal structure of the mine, but of the prejudices and negative stereotypes whites hold of them. They react by developing two social worlds, the 'public' one in which they interact with whites deferentially, attempting to survive economically and keep out of 'trouble', and the 'private' world of strong group cohesion, emphasizing mutual aid, protection of each other against whites and generosity. Drinking together is an important ritual of brotherhood. Loyalty to the Brothers is a consciously cultivated value.

Etiquette for relating to whites emphasizes deference,

formality and doing as one is told. One must, for example, laugh at a white's joke even though it involves pushing around a black Brother. In private, however, the white's behavior is acknowledged as callous and degrading. Blacks do not accept the legitimacy of the whites' stereotypes of them, but they make use of them on occasion to ingratiate themselves, to get favors from a patron.

Despite the workers' counter-culture, there is a good deal of loneliness and alienation among workers at the mine. In their situation of hard work and material deprivation, many workers fantasize about 'going home' as their central life interest. The Brotherhood culture is primarily a coping strategy, a 'local anaesthetic' for the hardships of life in a closed compound.

In such a situation, it is understandable that the workers' chief form of overt protest might well be desertion – leaving clandestinely before the expiry of a contract. But, in addition to coping sub-cultures and desertion, Van Onselen and others have demonstrated the widespread occurrence of such informal forms of resistance as theft from employers, failure to perform a given amount of work ('loafing'), poor quality of work, feigning illness and destruction of mine property.[25]

One cannot conclude, however, that all protest within mine compounds has taken this hidden and indirect form. There has, in fact, been an impressive history of more overt action. Although desertion remained the chief form of protest on the gold-mines of the Rand until 1913, there were numerous smaller riots, work stoppages and confrontations.[26] Those in 1901–2 took place in the context of transition from war-time to reconstruction, under circumstances of wage reductions, a decline in the purchasing power of workers' wages and a rapidly rising death-rate among black miners. In addition, the expectations of miners had been raised as a result of the ending of the War. Finally, they took place in the context of an offensive by the Randlords designed to curb the free movement of workers, particularly desertions.[27] In 1913, with the example of striking white miners before them, something like 9,000 black miners across the Rand struck over a period of three days. The years of World War I were also a period of black unrest on the Rand, culminating in the large strike of 1920, in which nearly half of the black work force participated at some stage.[28] A similar history of unrest can be found on Southern Rhodesian mines before the depression, the largest and best organized being that at the Shamva mine in 1927. While most of these early strikes were unsuccessful, Van Onselen himself comments that their organization was a considerable achievement, since they took place within two decades of the inception of the industry and in an extremely labor-repressive system.[29] The compound system could not, in the long run, suppress or prevent worker protest.

What was the role of the migrant, as opposed to the more stabilized workers, in these early strikes? Both kinds of worker participated in the actions, but it appears that the presence of the more experienced 'long-service' workers made the larger strikes possible, and that these workers tended to be in the leadership. I. R. Phimister has argued for the Shamva strike that two factors help explain why such a comparatively large and well-organized strike took place at this early point in time: the homogeneity of the work force in terms of proletarianization, and the presence of many 'long-service' workers at this mine. The proportion of workers from heavily proletarianized areas such as north-eastern Rhodesia (Zambia) had been increasing prior to the strike, in relation to the proportion of local Rhodesians. The average length of service in the 1920s for 60% of these workers was estimated at from eight to ten years. Even more important, the strike leaders had an average length of employment (including breaks in service) of six and a half years, and four of them had been there no less than 12–14 years. The leaders were industrial workers, not clerks or supervisors; particularly active were the 'hammer men', whose work on the open stopes was quite dangerous. Though virtually all of the 3,500 workers participated in the strike, the leadership came from among the more proletarianized.[30]

The 1935 strike on the Zambian Copperbelt sheds additional light not only on the role of migrants, but also on the role of the more 'open' compounds. In May, 1935, a series of strikes by all workers at Mufulira, Nkana and Roan Antelope mines broke out; they were the first efforts at collective action on the Copperbelt. The proximate cause was an increase of 50% in the tax for urban Africans, but the larger context was that conditions on the mines had worsened steadily during the depression, and that the wage reductions made in those years had not been made good. Prices of goods were rising.

At Mufulira, the compound clerks spread the word about the tax increase and called for a strike. They sent letters to clerks at Nkana and Roan, urging them to stop work as well. The Mbeni dance associations and the Watch Tower religious movement also supported the strike. After two days, the arrest of eight leaders and the promise of a government investigation, the strikers went back to work.

As the news reached Nkana, it too went on strike, led by clerks and gang leaders. After the arrest of 75 leaders and the arrival of troops from Lusaka, the strike was broken. The most serious events took place a few days later at Roan, which up to then had been peaceful. As the strike took hold, police were called in and without provocation attacked both strikers and bystanders. Strikers fought back with stones, sticks and bottles, and police opened fire, killing 6 and wounding 22. As further troops arrived, the fighting was stopped, and meetings were arranged with district officers to discuss the workers' grievances of taxes, bad food, low wages and poor treatment.

Jane Parpart has argued that in this case the compound, far from being the repressive institution that it may have been elsewhere, was a positive factor in the creation of class consciousness. Since housing was not divided ethnically, but rather by seniority and family size, workers of all groups mixed. The presence of women and children encouraged social life. A common language, 'town Bemba', evolved. In addition, when it came to concerted action, the compound facilitated it. Its compactness enabled information to spread quickly. Meetings could be called, such as those held on the football field, to air grievances. Organizers stood at strategic routes, funneling people to meetings. Posters went up all over the compound for those who could read.[31]

As in the Shamva strike, the more skilled and stabilized workers were the leaders in the strike. In general, the Zambian mine-owners' commitment to a policy of encouraging some stabilization of workers was an important factor behind the strike, as Parpart and others have pointed out. The 1935 strike was most serious at Roan Antelope, where there was a higher percentage of skilled workers, such as hoist drivers and blasting-license holders, than at the other two mines, and where the work force had a substantially lower turnover rate and a higher dependent population.[32] On the other hand, the unskilled, more 'migrant' workers joined in the labor actions with vigor and conviction. They were part of the large strike of 1940, and most of them supported the first African Mine Workers' Union within a few years of its establishment. Thus, as Parpart has put it, the working and living conditions on the mines had a strong impact on all black workers. A common subjugation to corporate authority, the visible gap between

Europeans and Africans and the example of the European union, all made for a certain community of interests among black miners in the period before 1953.[33]

Charles Perrings has used the occasion of the 1935 strike to make a slightly different point, the importance of looking at events in the rural economy to explain migrant-worker protest.[34] He argues that the apparent leading role of the Bemba in the strike can best be explained by reference to the fact that they had recently suffered a setback in their rural produce trade because of the closing of the Katanga border. Although the evidence as to the leading role of the Bemba in this strike is rather slim, and although it is not clear that the Bemba were in a much worse rural situation than a number of other Zambian peoples on the mines, still, the general point Perrings makes is valid. However, there is no necessary contradiction between it and an explanation which stresses stabilization. In the case of the Bemba, both influences – the one stemming from proletarianization and the other from the work place – worked in the same direction, toward increasing worker consciousness.

In general, for the Zambian and other mines during the colonial period, work-place factors, such as compounds, stabilization, skill and pay structures and the great racial inequalities, worked together to overcome labor-market divisions based on differences in proletarianization, at least to some extent. This situation began to change in the 1950s, as skill and wage divisions widened. Technological advance, the success of Africanization, and the unionization of African workers all made for wider differentials between the highest- and the lowest-paid workers.

DOMESTIC WORKERS

By contrast to both dockers and miners, domestic workers experience a highly personalized form of work-place control. Their work sites are typically scattered and small-scale, since the majority are employed by private households. There are many gradations of skill and pay, and of proletarianization. All these conditions might seem to militate against overt collective action by workers against their employers. But the amount of worker resistance by domestics has been greatly underestimated. Informal, individualized protest has been the most common form, but there have also been cases of collective action. By the 1950s, throughout Africa, many Domestic Workers' Unions had been formed, although today they often represent only a fraction of all such workers, usually only those employed by restaurants and hotels.

Domestic workers provide an example of an occupation in which the larger context of urban communication systems was able to compensate to some extent for the divisions stemming from the dispersal of work places. Although much of the work is quite privatized, domestics are by no means cut off from outside influences. In the early twentieth century in Lourenço Marques, domestics gathered several times a day to draw water at the public fountains. Similarly they queued up at the bakery, and there were always groups of them doing their errands at the post office and in the municipal markets. The shop talk in such places, the exchanging of information about jobs, wages and conditions, greatly diminished the structural isolation of domestics.[35] In Nairobi in the 1970s, the gatherings in residential neighborhoods, while walking babies or hanging out the laundry, served a similar intelligence function.[36]

Domestics were one of the earliest categories of Africans to stay for long periods of time in urban areas, and they often became subject to pass laws, registration and other labor-control measures. There is a notable history of resistance to such measures. In 1905–15 in Lourenço Marques, registration laws were imposed, but there was widespread non-compliance, and even a boycott in 1915, which led to numerous arrests. Domestics at this time comprised almost half of the African wage-labor force in Lourenço Marques.[37] In Nairobi in 1922, thousands of domestics joined the protest led by Harry Thuku against the *kipande*, or registration certificate, and wage decreases. By 1945 a new Houseboys Association protested against the *kipande*, the obligatory *Red Book*, and low wages. In Johannesburg between 1896 and 1914, forged and altered passes were a common form of defense among domestic workers. As in Kenya, employers wrote testimonials to their employees' character and trustworthiness on their passbooks when they left a job. One damaging comment, perhaps written in spite, could make it impossible for the worker to get another job, or could reduce his subsequent wages. In addition, having to carry a pass was experienced as a deep humiliation by the semi-skilled, upwardly mobile young men who became 'houseboys'. The system 'unleashed deep, passionate and destructive urges' in these men who were called 'boys'.[38]

As described further in Chapter 6, domestic workers are constantly confronted with the vast disparity in living standards between themselves and their employers. They often work long hours under close personal supervision. These aspects of their job cannot help but breed discontent. Responses such as high job turnover, theft, carelessness and breakage and 'laziness' are undoubtedly widespread among domestic servants, though it is difficult to provide a precise estimate of their extent. More straight-forward attempts to raise wages, whether individual or collective, could rarely succeed except in conditions of labor-market shortage. That domestics have not been unaware of changes in the demand for their services is suggested by events during World War II in Nairobi, when labor officers complained that domestic workers were 'exploiting' the shortage situa-

Migrants at the work place

tion by setting strict limits to the tasks they would do, and by accepting work only at increased wages. Officials lamented what they referred to as a new 'tendency to defiant behavior'.[39] Domestics, and the Domestic Workers' Association, were among the groups most heavily involved in the urban wing of the 1953 Mau Mau rebellion in Kenya.

Domestic workers do not have the same lengthy history of strike action as do miners and dock workers. It is difficult for strikes to be effective against a multiplicity of small employers, and in addition shortages of domestic workers, which might make a strike more effective, have been rare. Being only partly skilled, domestics can usually be fairly easily replaced. It is curious, however, that one of the few examples we have of organized urban social banditry mixed with crime occurred in Johannesburg and Durban in the early twentieth century, among young, poorly paid houseboys together with the unemployed. These were the armed 'Amalaita' gangs, who in addition to pass-forgery, burglary, house-breaking and other criminal activity, sometimes avenged injustices suffered by domestics at the hands of white masters or mistresses. They might jostle an employer off the sidewalk during the day, or make 'filthy remarks' at a white woman; in one celebrated case, they raped a white mistress against whom they had a grievance. Despite the criminality of much of their activity, these gangs can be seen as a form of worker economic protest. Amalaita groups were most active in periods when houseboy wages were falling. But perhaps too there is a deeper psychological meaning in their actions, as Van Onselen suggested when he termed them a veritable 'houseboys' liberation army, fighting to reassert its decolonised manhood'.[40]

The incidence of strikes and other forms of protest among dockers, miners and domestic workers makes possible some general observations as to when such actions are likely to occur and to be successful. First, the great majority of labor actions by migrants occurred at times of falling real wages or as a result of employer initiatives aimed at reducing wages. War and post-War inflation figured prominently as causes of the dock strikes in the 1940s, the 1901–2 and 1920 strikes on the Rand, the strikes between 1903 and 1912 in Southern Rhodesia, the post War strikes at Wankie colliery in 1918, 1919 and 1921, the gang activity of houseboys in Johannesburg before 1914 and the 1935 Copperbelt strikes. The only exception appears to be the 1927 Shamva strike, but here the evidence is not conclusive, and one of the chief grievances was pay relative to wages on the Rand.

Second, a factor that emerges as particularly crucial for the success of strikes by migrants (or indeed non-migrants) is their timing at periods of labor shortage, when labor supply was reduced. Since proletarianization was increasing throughout eastern, central and southern Africa throughout the colonial era, shortages tended to occur less and less frequently, and only at times when spurts of industrial development temporarily outpaced labor supply. Such situations placed workers in a much stronger bargaining position. This factor was important in the Shamva case, in strikes in Southern Rhodesia after 1918 in the wake of the Spanish flu epidemic and those between 1925 and 1928, in the assertiveness of domestic workers in Nairobi in 1945 and in the 1940 Copperbelt strike. Shortage, however, was not the situation in the 1935 Copperbelt strike, which came just after the depression, during which many workers had remained in town unemployed, since they lacked opportunities in the rural areas. And since shortage was not an important factor in the 1940s dock strikes, workers had to battle constantly against strike-breakers and strive to ensure that the strike was general throughout the town.

Rising expectations after periods of war-time hardship

were another important factor in many strikes, such as the dock strikes, the 1901–2 and 1920 Rand strikes and the Shamva strike. A final factor of specific importance to migrant workers was impositions of restrictions on mobility, making it more difficult to desert, to enter an urban area or to change jobs. Such initiatives were typically responded to in a more individualistic fashion, by evasion and deception, although there have been occasions of demonstrations and organizational protest against pass laws and registration schemes.

It appears, then, that labor action by migrants is affected by many of the same labor market forces that impinge on non-migrant workers. My main aim in this chapter, however, has been to show that, in addition, labor protest by migrants has been either facilitated or hindered by several kinds of work-place factors, such as the relative proportions of migrant and non-migrant workers, the degree of worker control through compounds, and the ease of communication among workers. Chapter 7 will return to the question of labor action among migrants, summing up its evolution over time and the effects of the decline of migration in some areas in recent years.

§ 6 §

WOMEN AS MIGRANTS AND WORKERS

Wage work in Africa has been, and largely still is, the province of men.[1] Of all those in wage employment, women form only about 10–15% in nations such as Kenya, Ghana and Zambia; this statistic is probably higher in South Africa, but lower in many less-developed areas. In this respect the continent as a whole contrasts with other parts of the Third World, particularly Asia and Latin America, where women are hired in larger numbers.

International capital hires women workers where they are cheap and also relatively docile. The kinds of international enterprises which demand cheap, factory-skilled workers – those engaged in assembly of complex consumer goods, such as electronics, printing, toys, clothing and footwear, for re-export to the developed world – have not yet been attracted to Africa in a big way. Such enterprises hiring women exist in only a few areas: Mauritius, Morocco and parts of southern Africa.

We suggest here that African women workers are not as cheap in relation to available male labor as elsewhere in the Third World, because of the generally low wages for unskilled males, due to the migrant tradition. In addition, African women workers are not necessarily docile. This consideration may help explain why labor-intensive processing industries have not yet located in Africa in great numbers, and why, when they do, they tend not to hire women, since there may be no marked cost advantage in doing so.

When labor is especially cheap, the costs of its reproduction must be borne elsewhere, outside the capitalist sector. In Asia and Latin America women work for low wages in part because their access to land has been more successfully restricted than in Africa. In addition, more of the total cost of reproducing the labor of women comes directly out of the (still low) wages of their husbands or fathers, because of the differing structure of the partriarchal household. Thus daughters are often sent out to work to supplement family income, but the wage they accept can be low, because it is not expected to provide full support for them or their children. In Africa, women's wages do not tend to be subsidized in this way. Women do, however, retain access to land in most areas. The land, though, does not function to subsidize their wages; it subsidizes those of men. Women cannot combine subsistence production and migrant labor as men do, because when a woman migrates there is no one left behind to work the land.

The historic pattern whereby women's work in the rural area was the *sine qua non* of male labor migration continues to inhibit women's incorporation into the labor force. It means not only that for many decades very few women have migrated from the rural areas, but also that those struggling to join the wage force have had to compete with migrant men who will also work for very low wages. Only where rural production, and therefore women's agricultural role, has been strongly undermined, as in southern Africa, have women been markedly incorporated into wage labor.

THE PROLETARIANIZATION OF WOMEN

Some authors have argued that the concept of proletarianization cannot be applied to women, or at least to women in Africa. Deborah Bryceson, for example, suggests that women cannot be said to have undergone a process of separation from the means of production because they never held possession or control of such means.[2] Iris Berger believes that the idea of women being semi-proletarianized carries with it the implication of strong psychological orientation to the family which is inconsistent with the evidence of active women's participation in workers' struggles in South Africa. The concept 'fails to distinguish adequately between the economic and the psychological aspects of women's roles'.[3] We will argue here that both these views are misguided, and that African women can be said to be experiencing a process of proletarianization similar to, but not identical to, that of men.

In a passage that is widely referred to and usually not fully appreciated, Marx writes that for workers to be available on the capitalist market they must be 'free' workers, free in a double sense:

> First of all, they must not themselves form a direct part of the means of production, must not belong to the means of production, as do slaves, serfs, etc. Secondly, the means of production must not belong to them, as the means of production belong to peasant proprietors.[4]

Taking the second kind of 'freedom' first, since that is the one most frequently emphasized, it is true that in most African pre-capitalist societies women did not have final disposition of or control over the land, the major means of production; but in agricultural societies women gained use-rights to land through marriage (and nearly every woman was married) or, in matrilineal societies, through the matrilineage. Though men usually allocated the land, they did not 'own' it individually; ownership, if there was such a concept, was communal. The custom was to provide each wife with land on which she was expected to grow food for herself, her husband and her children. In some societies she could sell extra produce from the land and keep the proceeds. In many societies women also had access to labor, in this context an even more important agency of production, through the labor of their children or their household slaves or through communal work groups. Thus women did have effective access to both land and labor, and many still do today. They can therefore be separated from these means and agencies of production in the same way as men can.[5]

However, a woman's *de facto* access to the means of production was, and still is, conditional upon her fulfillment of the demands of the patriarchal family. Thus she can lose such access through a second set of processes that have a specific impact on women, for example through divorce, desertion, barrenness or widowhood. But she may also, like men, see the productivity of her land decreased through overpopulation, land shortage, erosion, low crop prices, lack of labor and so forth, and these processes can proletarianize both women and men. When a woman migrates from the rural area as a result either of an intolerable family situation or of rural poverty, she has undergone a process of either partial or total separation from the means of production.

It is in the matter of pre-capitalist constraints on the disposition of their labor that women's situation is most different from that of men. This is Marx's first kind of 'freedom'; writing of men he says that the worker '... could not dispose of his own person until he had ceased to be bound to the soil; had ceased to be the slave, serf, or bondman of another ...'[6] Marx is writing of course only about production, but controls over women's freedom to dispose of their labor also apply in the arena of human reproduction. In African pre-capitalist societies women's labor was a critical part not only of production but also of reproduction. In both spheres they were responsible for a disproportionate amount of the labor, and they *were*, in a sense, part of the means of production and reproduction. Their status was not dissimilar to that of slaves or serfs. These kinds of pre-capitalist constraints must be partially broken in order to make possible any participation in wage labor. Breaking them is part of the process of proletarianization. And the constraints have to be fully broken if women are to compete equally with men in the wage-labor force.

Mere entry into wage labor does not automatically eliminate these constraints. Controls by male elders over women's mobility, sexuality and social life may be reduced, but the reproductive work of domestic labor, child bearing and child rearing continues. Until domestic labor is fully commoditized, or until it is equitably divided between men and women, there will be an imbalance in men's and women's total social labor burden, and this will differentially affect their relationship to the wage component.

Nor does wage work necessarily mean the lessening of family controls over the disposition of a woman's earnings. The demands of children, parents and other kin for money and support weigh heavily on working women. In contemporary urban Africa, patriarchal control manifests itself paradoxically in the tendency toward *reduction* of family financial responsibility by husbands, who insist that according to African 'tradition' it is the *woman's* responsibility to feed and clothe the children. A convention which made sense in a horticultural society, where women had use-rights to land, now legitimizes the subordination of women in a setting where the man is paid the wage and the woman usually has a lower wage or none at all, where high levels of divorce and desertion prevail, where polygyny is common and where urban expenses frequently outrun the resources of both men and women.

For these reasons women are typically *not* fully free workers in Marx's sense, especially when we include reproductive work in the analysis. A woman's subordinate position in the family too often constrains her participation in the work force, forcing her either to accept part-time or casual work, work that is close to home, work that requires less time-consuming education or training, or even to prefer self-employment because of the more flexible hours and work organization, which make it possible to combine it with domestic work. At the same time a woman *may*, of course, receive from a husband for her reproductive work, some financial or other support which will supplement her wage.

Thus, a woman's reproductive responsibilities may restrict her wage participation in a manner analogous to the way in which migrant males are constrained by their structurally enforced migrancy.[7] But if women get inadequate income or support for their reproductive work, they can be forced into full-time wage labor and are in this case just as much exploited as are men – perhaps more, since they carry a greater total labor burden. What the implications are for women's consciousness remains to be studied, but often they have fully identified with workers' struggles. South African women, for example, have been notably active in strikes and unions. This is surely because they are, in fact, more proletarianized than are women in other parts of Africa and other parts of the Third World.[8]

It is even more important in the case of women than of men to distinguish proletarianization – in the dual sense of the closing off of alternative means of making a living and of the breaking of pre-capitalist labor controls – from actual incorporation into the paid labor force. Capitalist development in Africa has in various ways undermined women's incomes from the land, and from pre-capitalist labor relations, but it has so far tended to push them into petty trade and self-employment rather than wage labor. Common roles for women in urban areas and mining compounds have been market trading, provision of cooked food, beer brewing and prostitution, all services for which male workers pay out some of their hard-earned wages. While these are undoubtedly functional for capital, in that they keep wage costs down, and for the women (many of whom make a good living in this way), in the long run these roles cannot provide economic security for large numbers of women. Large-scale marketing tends to be monopolized by men, and mass-market consumer goods tend to undermine women's craft and food-production services. The tightening of these urban options will tend further to proletarianize women.

FEMALE LABOR MIGRATION

Why do women leave the rural areas and come to town? It was a myth common among colonial officials and post-colonial planners that women came to town only with their husbands, and that female migration was simply a derivative of male migration. Historical studies of market women, lodging-house owners, and prostitutes suggest that this never was the case; certainly it is now so now. R. H. Sabot's analysis of female migrants to Tanzanian cities between 1950–2 and 1970–1 found that fully 33% of them were unmarried on arrival; they had come to town to find a job or a school. This percentage increased markedly from the 1950s;[9] and of the 160 women interviewed by Christine Obbo in Kampala in 1971, only 78 had come with their husband or followed him to town. 49 had come completely by themselves, and 15 had come to visit boyfriends or relatives, often in the capacity of housegirls.[10] On the other hand, female migration in West Africa still seems to take place predominantly in the company of husbands, the few independent migrants being older, widowed or divorced.[11]

The reasons women migrate can usefully be divided into two kinds: a) directly economic ones, such as inability to feed their families or obstacles to economic advance in the rural areas; and b) crises of family status, such as divorce, desertion, widowhood and unhappy marriages, which then result in women's losing economic support from their family. In most cases, the two kinds of reasons will be closely intertwined. Obbo interviewed 51 women who had migrated on their own, apart from men, from a variety of ethnic groups. 11 gave as their primary reason seeking a job or education or 'their fortune'; 8 came because of divorce, often coupled with childlessness; 15 came because of unsatisfactory marriages; 1 because of a sorcery accusation; 4 because of widowhood; and 12 because they were 'tired of village life' or 'tired of digging'.[12] Closer examination often reveals a combination of reasons: some widows said they had migrated because they had no land or had never fitted in with their in-laws. Sorcery accusations were often only an index to other problems: one woman had been bewitched by her husband's mistress, others had migrated to escape the stigma attached to divorces triggered by witchcraft accusations. Barrenness was also a reason for social stigma in the village, and sometimes led to divorce. But a childless couple might migrate because it was more possible to remain happily married in town.

Unhappy marriages are an important cause of migration, and often this involves escaping polygyny. In Kampala, many women felt it was better to live singly than to be married to a man who divided his time between several wives, and they tended simply to leave rather than seek a divorce in the traditional way. Among the Mossi in Upper Volta, marital difficulties likewise led to female migration, but here it was usually a question of discontent with arranged marriages.[13]

Economically, the will to migrate is sometimes less a case

of rural starvation than of obstacles to economic advance in the rural areas, including the jealousy of men and other villagers. In Kampala, the case of Lita, a successful Ganda shop-owner, whose stated reason for coming to town was 'to improve my business', is illustrative:

> She began by selling cigarettes and sweet bananas at home in Bulemezi county. Then she sold pens, books, and soda drinks. Finally she started selling sugar, salt and beer. Although her in-laws lived 23 miles away, they were angry at her business activity. Around that time her husband had a severe attack of malaria... she was accused of having used sorcery on him because she was allegedly jealous of the other woman her husband was seeing... [After she left] 'He begged me time and again to return to the village, but I had attained my goal and I was not going to abandon it.'[14]

Another case is that of Amina, a Lango woman, whose several ex-husbands had sabotaged her gin-distilling business in the rural area. She said she 'did not ever want to remarrry'.[15] Studies of women with some education have shown that they too, in addition to women in trade, are among the most likely to migrate independently, largely for reasons of economic opportunity.[16]

Even among those who come to town with their husbands, it must not be assumed that the woman is necessarily passive about the decision, or is completely economically dependent. In some instances in Kampala, it was more a case of the woman insisting on coming along; for example, Obbo was told that a trend among Rwandan migrants in the preceding ten years had been for wives, sisters and other female kin of male migrants to press to accompany them, since life in the village was increasingly difficult and the wages brought back were insufficient.[17] In town, married women often continued with or expanded businesses they had had in the village, as in the case of Filo, who had a hair-plaiting, bride-dressing, and dressmaking business, while her husband was a car mechanic and bicycle repairer.[18]

Women as migrants and workers

But economic factors can also force women who once migrated to town, with or without husbands, to retreat to the rural areas. In some cocoa-growing areas of Ghana, the decline of cocoa prices in the 1950s stimulated an increase in male labor emigration, and also in female emigration. Men brought their wives to work sites with them, and about two-thirds to three-quarters of the married male migrants had their wives with them. In this period too, women were able to find useful activities in town. But by the 1970s conditions in urban Ghana had deteriorated greatly, inflation was rampant and the rate of female migration had dropped. It became increasingly difficult to support families in town on meagre wages, or for women to subsist viably on self-employment. They were forced back on to subsistence farming to support themselves and their families, and in the 1970s were even sending food to the men in the towns.[19]

In some parts of Africa, particularly central and southern areas, rural economic decline proceeded in such a way as to have a particularly deleterious effect on some categories of women. Maud Muntemba has described how in Kabwe Rural District in Zambia, congestion and land shortage in the Reserve led to women's matrilineal inheritance rights being challenged, some widows no longer getting the access to the best lands that they had before. Such agricultural development as there was took place with ox-ploughs, and was, as in many cash-crop development areas, dominated by men. Colonial extension services channeled new agricultural technology to men, bypassing women. As a result, there was widespread migration of women to the mine compounds, where they engaged largely in self-employment.[20] Rural poverty is even greater in present-day Botswana, where conditions are similar to those described in Chapter 2 for Lesotho. A survey of one village found that 25% of the women were employed for wages – comparatively, a rather high proportion.[21] Most of this employment is available only in towns within Botswana, since neighboring South Africa has officially excluded 'foreign' migrant women.

Despite the legal obstacles, South Africa is the area where women's migration to towns has probably been the greatest, because of the overall rural impoverishment. In the first half of the twentieth century, women took advantage of certain legal loopholes in the pass system and migrated to towns in fairly large numbers. Their numbers in town increased faster than did those of men. From 1911 to 1960 the number of men in towns increased five times compared to a fifteen-fold increase for women. By 1960 the sex ratios in many South African towns had come into balance: for example, in East London in 1955 the ratio was 95 males to 100 females, and this despite an official apparatus designed to prevent such urbanization.[22]

Among the Xhosa by the 1930s, widows and young single women were particularly likely to migrate. What few land rights a widow might expect from her late husband's family became vulnerable to stiff competition from her own sons and from in-laws. Where rights could be claimed, envious relatives might still make life intolerable. Even a widow's own family became reluctant to accept her back, since she was yet another person competing for scarce land.

With the increasing incidence of pre-marital pregnancy, many young single women were also viewed as family liabilities, unlikely to bring in the traditional *lobola*, or bride price. Girls themselves often acted to defy the system of arranged marriages, and of polygyny, preferring to choose a partner on the basis of personal attraction. Running away to towns enabled them better to control their personal lives, particularly if they had had a few years of mission education and could qualify for domestic jobs. In the towns, too, there were more men who might be willing to help support them. Many such women remained in town on a permanent basis.[23] Women's migration here, then, took place for many of the same reasons that were noted above for other parts of Africa.

Just as male labor migration undermined the power of the elders in African pre-capitalist economies, so did female migration – to an even greater extent. George Chauncey has pointed out that among the Bemba in Zambia in the 1930s, townward migration by women not only further undermined an already weakened system of agricultural production, but also cut off the very basis of elders' control over young men, their control over marriage.[24] In the matrilocal village, the elder men depended on the labor of their wives and daughters, and on the bride-service labor of their in-marrying sons-in-law, to keep up agricultural production. A young man had to work in the village for ten years or more, primarily on his father-in-law's gardens, before he gained full rights to his wives and children. Male labor migration severely undercut this system, as male labor became scarce and men commuted their bride service to cash payments. But elders saw the migration of women as an even greater threat.

Elders protested vociferously against the mining companies' policy of administratively certifying relationships as 'marriages' for the purpose of allocating housing. The companies were attempting to encourage a large and stable supply of male labor in this way, but the elders protested that it encouraged couples to avoid all of their bride-service obligations to the older generation. They wanted to reassert their authority over the movements of women, to prevent them from 'becoming prostitutes'.

Women, therefore, often had to struggle against strong odds to achieve the right to migrate. In addition to getting away from home a woman had to establish herself in town. Often this required considerable ingenuity. On the Copperbelt a woman had to find a 'husband' in order to secure herself as a registered resident of the compounds. This was relatively easy, and temporary 'Copperbelt marriages' flourished. Women found people to pose as relatives in order to get their 'marriages' registered at the Urban Court. Forged documents were common. Thus registered, the couple could qualify for married housing, a great improvement over the bachelor quarters. If a man's 'wife' left, he could probably quickly find another, or just a succession of girlfriends, and still keep his married quarters. From the woman's point of view, such temporary marriages were often the starting-point in a process of bettering themselves economically through a series of boyfriends. Changing partners was a major avenue of upward mobility for women in the relatively high-wage context of the Zambian Copperbelt.[25]

This process, however, was exactly what elders were determined to prevent.[26] Often they would visit the compounds to inspect the conditions, at the invitation of the mine managers, who hoped to spur further male migration. Sometimes the elders would also search for women and attempt to return them home forcibly, but in this they were not assisted by the mine managements. When a Ngoni official at a meeting in the Roan Compound in 1937 ordered all Ngoni women 'without proper marriages' to return home, his remarks were 'met by mumbles of dissatisfaction from the women present'. When word spread that he might actually seize unmarried women, many of them temporarily fled into the township. The Lamba chiefs were especially persistent on this question, but found that, even when they succeeded in forcibly returning women to the village, the women simply fled to the compounds again. One Lamba chief lamented in 1943: 'We are always collecting these women from the Compounds and taking them back to their homes, but they run away again to the towns. We do these inspections, but the Europeans do not help us.'[27]

Women as migrants and workers

The chiefs and the rural Native Authorities in Zambia were, by themselves, unable to stem the flow of women to the compounds. But by the end of the 1930s their position was strengthened when increasing government concern over the deterioration of the rural areas led to a change in government policy in favor of assisting in the control of unattached women. Now Native Authorities could require women to obtain marriage certificates, without which they could not travel to urban areas unless given special permission. Fines were imposed, and several roadblocks were put up at bridges and other strategic points, staffed with police, to apprehend women traveling illegally. But women continued to resist, frequently forging passes or bribing men who drove trucks, who either claimed the women to be their wives or hid them during the search. Enforcement and legal problems beset the control system, and mining companies refused to require the women visitors to present passes. Although the exodus of women from the rural areas was probably slowed somewhat, it was not effectively stopped.

By contrast to Zambia, in South Africa mine-owners never encouraged the stabilization of black labor, and thus never allowed women in the compounds. In urban areas, though, the pass laws were not specifically applied to women until many years after they were imposed on men. And the application of them to women did not come without a long and heroic movement of opposition from women.

The Orange Free State was one of the first to attempt to impose pass laws on women. In 1912 a militant campaign of petitions and passive resistance was fought against this attempt.[28] In Blomfontein in May, 1913, a crowd of some 600 shouting and threatening African women marched past police to the Town Hall, and handed over sacks full of unwanted passes. 34 women were arrested. The resistance spread to other towns; 52 were arrested at Jaggersfontein, 800 beseiged the Town Hall at Winburg, and in other towns imprisonments totalled at least 200. Although the resistance quieted with the outbreak of war in 1914, it did not succeed in getting the Orange Free State to rescind its pass laws for women, though the Union government did exert some pressure on it to administer them more lightly.

Agitation against passes for women surfaced again in 1923, when the Union was considering a new Urban Areas Act, and served to convince parliamentarians not to extend the Orange Free State system throughout the Union. It broke out again in 1930 in the city of Durban when the Union was considering allowing municipalities to issue permits to women, making their entry conditional on their joining a husband or father who had been working for two years continuously. Women living in the Durban Women's Hostel were enraged upon reading about the proposed amendment and, led by Bertha Mkhize, a tailor's assistant, over 200 of them marched to the city hall and persuaded the local magistrate to promise that this provision would not be enforced in Durban. And when, after the Nationalists came to power in 1948, and announced in 1953 that reference books would be issued to women beginning in 1956, years of nation-wide protests, demonstrations and riots by African women ensued.[29] But these failed; by the 1960s the policy of breaking up families where the husband and wife had different qualifications to remain in urban areas became a harsh reality, and mass removals of women, children and the aged to 'homelands' began.

WOMEN AS WORKERS

Many African women have struggled to free themselves from the constraints of the pre-capitalist rural household. The wage sector of capitalism, on the other hand, has absorbed them only in a very limited way. Considering only formal-sector wage employment – and excluding self-employment in trade, in which African women have been so active – there are only two areas of Africa where employment of women is marked. One is South Africa and the associated areas of Botswana, Lesotho, and other border areas, and the other is where the development of commercial agriculture has provided employment, in places such as the southern Cameroon, Kenya or Zimbabwe. As a percentage of all wage employment, women workers in 1970 were about 14% in Kenya, about 10% in Ghana and about 6.7% in Zambia.[30] For South Africa, wage-labor-force figures are unavailable, but in 1970 nearly one-quarter of the whole economically active population, African and white, was accounted for by African women.[31] Where female wage-labor participation is low is either in quite undeveloped areas such as Guinea–Bissau or Mali, in areas where women's economic contribution has been primarily in trade, such as parts of West Africa, or in areas with strong Islamic influence, such as the Sudan, northern Nigeria and parts of the East African coast.[32]

Women who have wage jobs are usually a small minority of all women defined as 'economically active'. Included in this concept are all those who are at work for pay or profit during a specified reference period, or who are looking for such work. However, women's total economic contribution, including subsistence production, unpaid domestic labor and occasional trade, is far greater than that reflected in this somewhat arbitrarily defined term.[33] Percentages of women economically active in 1970 vary from highs of 46% and 49% in Botswana and Lesotho to lows of 5% and 7% in Angola and the Sudan. West African nations are also high on this measure; for example, 32% were economically active in Ghana, 47% in the Ivory Coast.[34]

The great majority of wage-earning women throughout Africa work in agriculture. But the picture varies: on the low side there is Ghana, where in 1971 only 11.5% of all women wage workers were in agriculture; on the higher side is Kenya, where 36.1% were.[35] Higher still is South Africa, where in 1970 agriculture accounted for 43.9% of the female labor force.[36] These figures reflect women employed in commercialized, export-oriented agriculture, such as rubber, coffee, tea and sisal plantations, operated by companies such as the Cameroon Development Corporation in West Africa, white farmers, as in South Africa and Kenya, or even African-owned large-scale farming, as in Kenya. In areas such as Zambia, Botswana and Lesotho, the percentage of women reported working for wages in agriculture is much lower, since farming is small-scale and relatively undeveloped, and women's role, though major, is not as wage employees.

In most areas women are greatly underrepresented in relation to men among mine, transport and industrial workers. In the latter category, however, some industries represent exceptions, and factory work is in some areas a growing field for women. Two industries where great numbers of women have been employed are first-stage agricultural processing and garments and textiles. In East Africa, for example, women are employed in tobacco processing, coffee-bean sorting, milling and cleaning, sisal decorticating and brushing, sugar extracting and refining, tea sorting and cotton ginning. In Ghana in the garment industries, perhaps 30% of the skilled and unskilled workers are women, and women are also in the printing trades in sizeable numbers.[37] And in Ethiopia where a newly developing small textile industry is important, in the 13 largest public, private and cooperative firms over 50% of the workers are women.[38]

South Africa, though, is the major area of female factory employment. This has been true since the 1930s in garment, textile, footwear and food-processing industries, and in recent years multinational investment in a variety of areas has brought increasing employment of women. In the 1930s and 1940s it had been predominantly white and colored women in such factories, but by the 1960s white women were moving into white-collar work, leaving factory work to blacks. The need to hold the line on wages led to the hiring of black and coloured women by the 1940s in the garment factories, and by the mid-1960s in the textile factories. In general, by the 1960s a spurt of industrial growth had greatly increased the demand for factory workers, and those African women who had relatively secure residential status in the urban areas were able to move into the breach. In these areas, factory work was an advance for African women compared to the chief alternative, domestic work. It offered fewer constraints on family life, because of shorter hours and off-site living arrangements, and paid a wage from two to four times higher.[39]

Between 1960 and 1970, the percentage of women among African production workers doubled, from 3.1% to 7.4%.[40] By 1981, 105,168 African women were employed in industry, a 133% increase since 1969, compared to an increase of only 47% for Asian and colored women.[41] On the other hand, many new garment, textile and other factories were located in the rural homelands or in adjacent border areas, where they drew on destitute, proletarianized rural women for whom even wages below the poverty datum line represented an advance.

Women form a large portion of the work force in these 'border industries', which were developed as a way to minimize travel distances of migrant workers, keeping them further from the heartland of South Africa, and also to preserve low wages and low skill levels. Wages in these industries have been shockingly low. In 1974 and 1975 Kool Look Wigs (in the area of Babalegi in Bophuthatswana), which employed about 600 workers, mostly women, was the subject of a press exposé on this account. It was found that the basic wage was R4 a week and the average R6 a week. There was no pension fund, medical assistance, transport allowance or paid sick leave. The Poverty Datum Line at this time in Babalegi was R18 a week.[42] That so many workers accepted such wages testifies to their desperation and lack of alternatives.

As noted earlier, men predominated among domestic workers in Africa during the colonial era, but this area of work has become increasingly feminized as women have gained access to the skills required, often through classes in European cooking, sewing, hygiene and languages sponsored by mission schools, welfare centers and women's organizations. As more urban Africans have come to be able to afford domestic help in eastern, western and central Africa, these workers have become predominantly women. One 1979 study of a middle-income African area of Nairobi, for example, found that 95% of the domestic servants were women, usually young girls between the ages of 15 and 20.[43] Men still predominate in the more highly paid positions in the field, such as cooks, drivers, hotel and restaurant workers and employees of European families. South Africa, however, has a longer tradition of women as domestic workers. Of all domestic servants in South Africa in 1970, fully 78.7% were African women. Of the total economically active female population, 36.8% were in the service sector, which consists mainly of domestic workers.[44]

In the early phases of industrialization throughout the world, jobs requiring literacy and training – clerical work, medical work, teaching – usually go to men. As more lucrative jobs open up elsewhere in the economy for men, as the medical, educational, welfare and other institutions expand so that lower-level jobs are created within them, and as women gain access to education and appear in the labor market as a low-wage alternative to men – at that point such occupations as nursing, lower-level teaching, and typing, secretarial and clerical work tend to become rapidly feminized. Such has been the case in Africa.

Until about the mid-1950s in eastern, central and western Africa, white-collar work, like domestic work, was the almost exclusive preserve of men. Since then women's participation in these areas has been growing, at least in eastern and central Africa. Clerical work is not yet so completely feminized as it is in Western societies, and teaching is more highly feminized at the primary level than it is at the secondary. Men still predominate in clerical work in West Africa and among Africans in South Africa.[45] But in almost all countries a closer look at the lower clerical categories of typist and stenographer usually reveals female predominance. In Kenya in 1976, for example, some 89% of secretarial workers were female.[46]

As Ilsa Schuster has argued for Zambia, the entry of women into urban clerical jobs is an example of a successful government policy for the incorporation of women in development.[47] For these few 'sub-elites', many of whom are young and unmarried, development can mean progress. The inherent disadvantage, however, has been seen in Western societies: the ideological sex-stereotyping of women into clerical, nursing and teaching roles which prevents their advance into other economic positions.

In Zambia, the 'sub-elite' stratum emerged after 1964, during the first decade of independence, as a result of new educational and manpower training programs. As the development focus shifted from the Copperbelt to Lusaka in the 1960s, so did female migration. Compared to the restricted job opportunities for women prior to this time, the new educational expansion made possible a tremendous advance. Between 1964 and 1969 there was a 280% increase in the number of girls attending secondary school in the country.[48] Whereas in 1966 only 14 women obtained clerical jobs through the employment exchange in Lusaka, by 1973

453 did.[49] Schuster emphasizes that the 20 office workers she studied in Lusaka enjoyed modern housing and sanitation, high salaries, secure, undemanding jobs, and fewer children through access to birth control. The secretaries, cashiers and typists earned from K78 to K290 a month, whereas a beer brewer could earn only K18 to K40 and women cleaners about K28 a month.[50]

In all African nations, the percentage of women in actual elite positions – in professional, technical and managerial occupations – is very low. Only some 2–3% of the economically active female population was in this category in Ghana and Zambia in 1970, as opposed to some 5–6% of the male labor force. In South Africa, on the other hand, the pattern is a little different. African women have actually had more access to the professions there than have African men, through their entry into nursing and teaching, so that in 1970 2.7% of the African female labor force was in this category, and only 1% of the African males.[51] In all countries, the two occupations of nursing and primary school teaching account for a very large proportion of African professional women. The percentage of women in administrative and managerial occupations is even lower than in professional jobs, and the male/female gap there is particularly wide.

CONSCIOUSNESS AND PROTEST

If we confine ourselves to the more obvious and visible manifestations of worker consciousness, such as strikes and trade union membership, we are likely to miss the full extent of women's struggles in the labor force, and we would be guilty of the same mistake for which van Onselen chided historians writing about male laborers.[52] Women's struggles as workers have been as varied in form, if not in extent, as those of men, and have ranged from the individual to the collective, from desertion, theft and 'laziness' to demonstrations, strikes and trade union activism.

In relation to the labor market women's struggles have actually taken two discrete forms. First are those just mentioned which are undertaken by women who are workers; these are the same *kinds* of actions as those undertaken by male workers. Second, there are those actions which are common to nearly all women, workers or not, who depend for some support on the wages earned by men; these strategies involve securing access to wages formally earned by men. Women are subordinated both in the labor market and in the realm of reproduction. The first subordination – low wages, lack of education or jobs – forces them to look for support in the second arena, the household and family. Here we find strategies which vary from, at one extreme, support for men which enables them to earn more wages and which includes logistic and material support for men who are engaged in strikes, to, at the other extreme, pressures on men to ensure that a portion of their wages goes to the support of women and children. These strategies in the reproductive realm are most often engaged in individually, but collective action and outside social pressure are often brought to bear.

No neat classification of these two kinds of actions as 'class' *versus* 'gender' forms of solidarity is adequate. Even in the 'class' actions by workers, the specific grievances of women workers are often different, owing to differing positions in the work force. On the other hand, gender solidarity is often only made possible by the fact of similar class position and, conversely, is often undercut by class differences. The class and gender systems interpenetrate in complex ways.

Jane Parpart's study of women in the mining compounds on the Zambian Copperbelt nicely illustrates the situation of women who, while excluded from the wage jobs, were nevertheless an active force in pressing both for higher wages for men and at the same time for a guarantee of their own share of the paycheck. After the mines opened in the mid-1920s, women began migrating there in large numbers, as described above. Many of them stayed for a very long time. By 1943 in one mine township, Nkana, 33% of the women had been there for three years or more, and many had not visited home since their initial migration.[53]

Women were important contributors to the major Copperbelt strikes of 1935 and 1940. They joined in, supplying food from their gardens, cheering on strike leaders, marching in picket lines, and attending union meetings after the establishment of the African Mineworkers Union in 1949. In addition, a key axis of interrelation between the women and mine administrators involved the issuing of food rations; since these were often given to the registered wives of workers, the women's complaints about shortages could and did lead to quarrels between them and mine officials, sometimes resulting in riots.

Broadly speaking, women on the mines recognized the antagonism between management and workers and supported the workers. They are also reported to have pressured their husbands to remain loyal to the union in the mid-1950s, when a rival staff association was being formed. At least one worker is said to have switched back to the union from the association because 'my wife used to quarrel with me for not attending union public meetings'. She forced him to attend because all her friends were laughing at her and calling her husband an informer.

In this sort of initiative, women were identifying with the class of their husband, even though they as individuals were not members of it, on the presumption that that is where their own support would come from. A similar stirring example of such female support for male workers' struggles can be found in the long 1947 rail strike in French West Africa. Women's food-supplying role there was critical.[54]

Other strategies are necessary, though, when support from males is in jeopardy, as it so often is for African women. Women's attempts to get a share of the wages encompass many activities, from the entrepreneurial sale of food, beer, lodging and sex, to pressures on their boyfriends or husbands to give them money for clothes or child support. To think of such affairs as 'mere' lovers' quarrels and marital spats does not do justice to the seriousness of what is frequently at stake: economic support. All personal relations between men and women inevitably become colored by the inequities of differential relation to the capitalist labor market.

The commercialization of services such as food, beer and sex has been for many women quite a successful way to get access to the collective pay check, both in Zambia and throughout Africa. And on the Copperbelt in the 1940s even adultery paid: women were in such high demand that married women sometimes sold sexual favors on the side in order to get a little extra cash. Despite such efforts, they remained dependent on the generosity of their husbands. Most women on the Copperbelt, like many African wives, did not know how much their husbands earned, and made it known that they wished they did.

When personal importuning or neighborhood pressure did not work, women even turned to the authorities for help – the very ones they struggled against on other issues. In a number of cases, wives requested the Tribal Representatives to force their husbands to give them more money. The elders, advocates of marital stability and traditional obligations in this new setting, frequently did press miners to give 'responsible' wives some of their paycheck. After the Tribal Retainer system was abolished in 1953, women turned to the personnel departments and social workers for assistance. Most were sympathetic, especially after one doctor's finding in the mid-1950s that malnutrition had risen among the families of men on an all-cash, no-rations wage. The men, for their part, were frequently afraid of being fired if their wives continued to push their complaints through the hierarchy of welfare officials, and so complied.

The last-ditch option for a woman in a case of inadequate support was separation or divorce, and the Copperbelt was one context in which that made sense: it was fairly easy to find another partner in the 1930s and 1940s, when the male:female ratio was about 2:1. Whether changing partners always resulted in a more financially secure arrangement is surely open to doubt; but there was always hope, and in this very fluid situation of often temporary marriages women were free to try their luck.

In this context, where men had relatively high wages, there were apparently fewer women who rejected marriage altogether, as did a number of those independent entrepreneurs interviewed by Obbo in Kampala. Like successful entrepreneurs, women who are within the paid-labor force in higher-paying clerical positions may also be more likely to reject marriage as an option, preferring to live from their own earnings.[55]

As members of the wage-labor force, women have a reputation for docility which, in South Africa at least, they ill deserve. Women's consciousness as workers is inevitably colored by their relation to the reproductive sphere.[56] But 'family ties' may operate either to lessen proletarianization, as when the woman's wage is merely a supplement to the family income, or to increase women's dependence on wage labor, as in a case such as South Africa, where many family members are almost solely dependent on each female worker.

The first case examined below, that of women domestic workers in South Africa, illustrates that class (and class–race) consciousness can be very high among African women. This is so in the sense that they perceive their own exploitation, feel a community of interest with others who are similarly exploited and understand the situation as one of black/white and capital/labor conflict. They feel very powerless, however, and have only been able to act collectively on their perceptions in a limited way. The second case examined, that of women factory workers in the garment and textile industries, shows that, under different conditions, women who are similarly proletarianized and similarly exploited can and have acted collectively to change their situation.

How do women domestic workers in South Africa feel about their work? A study of Jaclyn Cock of a random sample of 225 domestic workers in an area of the eastern Cape concludes that the vast majority 'do not accept the legitimacy of their own subordination in the social order. On the contrary, they have a high consciousness of exploitation.'[57] They complained of

The low status of the occupation: 'We get no respect.' 'Educated people look down on us domestics.'

Lack of appreciation by employers: 'Your employer looks down on you. You have to keep on saying, "Remember that I am a woman too."'

Low wages: 'You work very hard and earn very little.' 'It's hard work, very little money, and makes you tired.'

Long hours: 'We have to leave our children early in the morning and look after our madam's children. We have no time to look after them even when they are sick.'

Lack of pension rights or job security: 'You work for years and get nothing at the end. Not even thank you.' 'You can't complain or you might lose your job. If you complain your employer tells you about all the girls coming to the door looking for work.'

'I even have to look after the dogs and cats. The employer thinks about them more than they think about me..'[58]

As to the work itself, not one of the respondents said that she enjoyed her work or derived any sense of satisfaction from it. Most said they found the work boring rather than interesting, and about half said they were not learning any useful skills on the job. Some felt they were learning, but that such skills as making sweets, cakes and cold drinks were of no use to them because they did not have the money to buy them for their own families: 'Yes, I have learned how to cook and roast the meat that I cannot eat.' All workers said they had too much work to get through during the day, and over one-third felt their employers supervised them too closely, bossing them around: 'She tells me to do one hundred things a day.'[59]

The domestic worker is constantly exposed to a standard of living she can never attain, to material things she can never have. Under some conditions this might lead to a 'deferential worker' who is content to look up to her employer, but in most cases the vast gap in living standards cannot help but lead to extreme frustration. In South Africa there is a usual mask of deference, but not far below the surface are feelings of either anger or depression. Of the domestic workers interviewed, 90% expressed anger or indignation and 10% expressed sadness. All of them, therefore, felt strongly on this issue. 'It makes me angry especially when I have to serve her tea in bed and she is younger than I am' (a 65-year old worker). 'It makes me angry to look at their gardens and the food they buy for their dogs. It is better than they buy for us.' 'It makes my heart break ... The money she gives me is not even as much as her pocket money.' All the domestic workers in the depth sample thought they should be paid more: half thought they should be getting twice as much as they were; many thought three to five times as much. They also complained of discrimination on the job as women: they were paid less than men and got no maternity benefits.[60]

Cock's study graphically underlines another oppressive aspect of domestic service in South Africa, the deprivation

Women as migrants and workers

of family life that workers experience. All the workers in the depth sample had children, and in over half the sample the domestic worker was the sole breadwinner and support of her family. Often they leave at 5 a.m. and do not return until 7 p.m. Of the sub-sample of 50, the children of 12 workers were looked after by neighbors or paid caretakers, those of 12 others by 'no one', and those of another 25 by relatives, usually a grandmother or older child; often this older child is a daughter who is thus kept out of school in order to run the home. Maids are not allowed to bring their own children with them to work, and usually see them only after work, or once a week in the case of live-ins, or only a few times a year in the case of migrants.

The children of whites, on the other hand, are well cared for; one of the rationales for employing domestics is that it enables white women to devote more time to their children's intellectual and social development. Clearly this is done at the expense of black children.[61]

Another aspect of family stress is expressed in these worries: 'I have to sleep in and neglect my husband.' 'While we are at work other women can play with our husbands.' Family life is disrupted by the oppressive work regimen both of wives and of husbands, the latter frequently being migrant laborers in mines or other industries and themselves cannot get home very often. No wonder then that there is a high degree of marital instability: of the depth sample, 78% had been married but only 48% were still married. Many women complained about their husbands: 'We are badly treated. Our husbands are making it worse because they don't help us with their own children.' 'Our men won't tell us what they earn.' 'Men are useless these days, they spend all their money on drink.' 'My husband got a gratuity when he left the BAAB. He wouldn't tell me how much it was. He thought he was a king. He forgot that money will be finished. Now I am the only one who pays the rent, food, everything.' 'I am coping with nine children. My husband does not pay a cent.' 'They can take other girl friends even if they are married. We can't do that.'[62]

Many of the domestic workers expressed a deep sense of hopelessness and despondency about their own lives. Whatever hopes they had for the future were focussed on their children. One of the few compensations for such work was being able to educate their children. They themselves usually had a minimum amount of formal education, 63% having attended school, but three-quarters of these not beyond the primary level. They invested a considerable portion of their income in the education of their sons and daughters, in the hope that they would have a better life, perhaps in a white-collar job. This was also seen as a kind of insurance policy for themselves in their old age. In view of the low wages, sending children to school, or money to family in the bantustans, frequently represented a high degree of sacrifice and self-denial by women domestics.

The extreme deprivation of personal and social life, the long hours (84–5-hour weeks) and the burdensome supervision led Cock to compare domestic service to a Goffmanesque 'total institution'. In fact, an image commonly used by workers to describe themselves was that of slaves: 'Our employers should treat us like people and not like slaves.' The tightly scheduled daily routine, the unchallengeable authority of the employer, and the restriction of interaction outside the walls of the house, all contribute to such an image. Visitors are allowed only at certain hours, and sometimes visits from members of the opposite sex, even if they are husbands, are prohibited. The social distance between worker and employer is great, and interaction is formalized and bounded by special etiquette. Many madams address their servants in broken English at a slower pace and in a higher-pitched tone than usual. Servants must address their employer as 'madam' and 'master' in the eastern Cape, and must invariably be deferential in manner. They, on the other hand, are referred to as 'girl' or 'boy' and addressed by their first names in a manner befitting children. Most whites do not even know their servants' African surnames. Despite these parallels with a 'total institution', the individualized pattern of authority here is a difference, along with the fact that most domestics do have access to alternative definitions of the situation through family and neighbors and thus are able to evolve a critical consciousness.

Many writers have noted that deference shown by domestic workers in South Africa and other parts of Africa is usually more apparent than real. It is a mask, deliberately cultivated as necessary for success on the job. Cock writes that domestics in South Africa recognize their dependence on the existing structure of society but reject the legitimacy of the distribution of power and wealth in that structure. They adopt a mask of deference as a way of coping with their situation.[63] It is not a contradiction to say that, while keenly perceiving their own exploitation and denying its legitimacy, they at the same time generally try to remain on good terms with their employers in day-to-day relations.

The powerlessness of the domestic's situation seems to block much overt expression of dissatisfaction. But such strong feelings of discontent cannot remain completely hidden. Expression may be devious, even inadvertent, as in slow or careless work, or breakage of china and tools – problems of which many employers complain. There is also petty theft, which is said to be widespread. It would be surprising if the daily experience of the vast gap in living standards did not lead to some surreptitious attempts to redress the balance. In addition there have also been examples of collective protest, such as the widespread participation of women domestic workers in the demonstrations against the pass laws in the 1950s. One headline in the

Johannesburg Star in October 1958 read 'No Nannies Today' as 2,000 nannies stayed away from work to protest against the issuance of pass books;[64] both migrant and non-migrant domestic workers took part. And in the 1970s a Domestic Workers Association was formed, even though domestics and farm workers are still legally prohibited from forming recognized unions.

In some contrast to domestic workers, African women working in factories, particularly in the garment and textile industries, have been a very militant and politically active force in South Africa. They have been part of the increasing militancy of the black working class in South Africa in the 1970s and 1980s, stemming from low wages coupled with inflation, and the fusion of the nationalist and labor struggles. As in the case of men workers, the larger causes of their activism lie in their high degree of proletarianization and their oppressive work experiences.

The work situation of factory workers is different from that of domestic workers, and makes it easier for them to undertake collective actions. They work in groups in industrial settings, and in some cases even the ownership of the firms is highly centralized. The Frame Company, for example, is a vast industrial empire which in 1973 employed over 22,000 people in factories operating in South Africa (concentrated around Durban and in border areas and homelands), Zimbabwe, Zambia and Malawi.[65] Women work together with, if not on the same job level as, men and can participate jointly with them in strikes. In Durban and other areas, roughly half the female workers are migrants, and they reside in company-owned, single-sex hostels, crowded and rigidly controlled. Similarly to conditions in male mining compounds, these are not 'total institutions' where protest is vigorously repressed, but rather act as hothouses of discontent.[66]

Another factor conducive to protest in the garment and

textile industries is the high level of female membership in trade unions, which dates back to organizing efforts by white and colored women in the 1930s. Black women began becoming members of the previously white and colored Garment Workers Union in the 1940s. By 1953, due to apartheid legislation, black workers were forced to form a separate body, the National Union of Clothing Workers. By the 1960s it was the largest black union in the country, and primarily female, under the leadership in the 1970s of Lucy Mvubelo. In the 1950s trade union organizing for all blacks became subject to massive repressive legislation, and only by the 1970s did the legal situation begin to ease. By 1974 there were some 23 African trade unions, still unregistered, and nine of these had women as Secretaries-General.[67] By the late 1970s there were 27 independent African unions, but these were still non-registered and largely unrecognized by employers, despite strikes, such as that which occurred in October, 1978, when 250 black women struck against Britain's Ever Ready (SA) subsidiary after the company refused to recognize and negotiate with their union, the National Union of Motor Assembly and Rubber Workers of South Africa. Those unions that are being recognized are the 'parallel unions' affiliated to white unions, as in the tie between the white Garment Workers Union and the black National Union of Clothing Workers, which Douwes Dekker and others have characterized as a 'mother–daughter' relationship.[68]

In South Africa as a whole, there were waves of strikes during 1973–4, and 1980–1, and three widespread stay-at-homes following the Soweto uprising in 1976. The whole period from 1973 on was one of increasing militancy.[69] Women took a prominent part in these actions, and a detailed list of all the strikes they participated in would be impressive indeed. The issues were the classic ones: wages, long hours, unhealthy conditions, treatment on the job and union rights. Women's participation has been most marked in the textile and garment industries, where their numbers are highest. Women participated in the many Durban textile and clothing strikes in 1973; in stoppages by some 4,608 garment workers in Johannesburg in March and April, 1973; in the strike by some 1,800 workers in 20 garment factories on the Witwatersrand in February–March, 1982; and in another massive textile strike in Durban in 1980. Outside the textile industry, large strikes in which women alone were acting include a wildcat strike of 850 African women at Langeberg canning factory in East London in 1978 over overtime pay; a strike by 700 African women at Sea Harvest fish factory in Saldanha Bay in 1979 over pay, 12-hour work days, unhealthy conditions and union rights; and the Ever Ready strike noted above.

One important question, however, is the extent to which specifically female issues were addressed in these industrial actions. It appears that it is all too easy for women's issues to be submerged in larger struggles over general wage levels and union recognition. For example, in the textile industry a uniform policy had been instituted by the mid-1960s to pay women a wage about 20% lower than that of men, and implementation of this policy coincided with a large influx of women, so that by 1980 they constituted about 70% of all textile workers. Black women are also employed in the least-skilled, lowest-paying positions in the industry. Most supervisors are male, and women have little chance for advancement. In the textile strikes in Durban in 1973, the union had included in its early demands the removal of wage discrimination against women, but in the negotiations that occurred during the strikes this issue was forgotten. Even in the one case where it was actually raised, the workers eventually settled for a male minimum wage of R18 and a female one of R12 – at a meeting where intimidating car-loads of plain-clothes policemen were present.[70]

Women as migrants and workers

That such sex-based oppression is very much on the minds of women workers is supported by the interviews conducted by Westmore and Townsend among women workers in Durban in 1973. The women emphasized not only the high level of financial support they contributed to their families and their extra burden of domestic work, but also the way in which male supervisors at work harassed them sexually.[71] Even formal policies relating to women in textile factories are manipulative and degrading, as the following report shows:

> In the Frame factories, prospective female employees who survive a mandatory pregnancy test are then subjected to the continual watchful eye of factory doctors instructed to watch for signs of impending motherhood. Until early 1980 the Frame factories terminated the services of pregnant women, but since then an altered policy ostensibly provides for reemployment eight weeks after confinement. Women workers allege, however, that supervisors retain the arbitrary power to determine whether a woman will be reinstated. Those allowed to return are required to undergo a 'retraining' period (which the industry claims to be six weeks and the women claim is actually three months) during which time they are excluded from bonuses and overtime work. Instances of coercive intrusion by capital into workers' personal lives appear to be not uncommon in South Africa. In one engineering factory it was discovered in 1970 that African women were being forced to take the pill daily under a nurse's supervision.
>
> Other arbitrary and sometimes humiliating regulations dominated the lives of women textile workers... Company policy, for example, forbids them from using any company toilet paper or cotton scraps to supplement the single sanitary napkin they are issued. And, while men are frisked for company property at the end of each day, women must go through a special 'searching room' where they are more thoroughly scrutinized. Possession of trade union material found during these searches may provide grounds for dismissal.[72]

Recent workers struggles in South Africa have been aimed at challenging not sex discrimination in particular, but rather the whole oppressive system of low wages, heavy discipline, pass laws, migrant labor, residential segregation and denial of union rights from which all Africans suffer, both women and men. From the evidence we have, there appears to be a great deal of male–female cooperation in struggling against these conditions. Women, among the lowest-paid and least-skilled sections of the work force, doubly exploited because of their position in the household, have been ardent and purposeful supporters of worker action, sometimes even more so than men. They are highly conscious of their particular exploitation as women, but at the present juncture, with bare toleration of unionism for Africans and overwhelming oppression of blacks in all spheres of life, it appears that a coordinated struggle for rights of black workers in general is the only strategy which may have some success. Women's struggles have not been, and probably cannot be for some time, separated from the wider struggle against apartheid and capitalism.

§ 7 §

MIGRANTS, PROTEST AND THE FUTURE

We have considered migrant labor as a form of partial incorporation into capitalist production which came into being as a result of two factors: first, the need of capital for large numbers of cheap, low-skilled workers; and, second, specific features of pre-existing production systems in Africa. Migrant labor represents the articulation of two discrete systems of production, but is predicated upon the dominance of one. It requires either the political–military or commercial domination of capital to initiate and sustain the separation of large numbers of people from subsistence or peasant production in order to enter wage labor.

As part of a world-wide capitalist production system, migrant labor is congruent with a low organic composition of capital, the employment of relatively large numbers of workers with low skill levels, and a high turnover of workers between wage work and non-wage work. The system relegates a large part of the social cost of the reproduction of labor to the non-wage peasant or subsistence sector. As the technical and structural conditions for the accumulation of capital at the world level change, so do pressures arise for a change in the system of labor exploitation. Pressures may also emerge from struggles by workers themselves; for example, their demands for higher wages or better housing may force employers and the state to consider changes in the system of wage labor incorporation.

In the years following World War II, both a restructuring of capital and an upsurge in labor militancy and nationalist protest forced major modifications in the migrant labor system. Though the causes of this crisis were similar throughout Africa, the outcome varied from colony to colony, depending on the particular balance of political–economic forces. In this chapter we point to two contrasting forms of resolution of this crisis, in East and West Africa on the one hand and in South Africa on the other, and conclude with a consideration of the specific and continuing characteristics of migrant laborers as members of a discrete segment of the African working class.

THE TRANSFORMATION OF THE MIGRANT SYSTEM

After World War II the trend toward investment of international capital in secondary industry in the Third World, rather than exclusively in raw material extraction, began to make itself felt in Africa. The market situation of multinational firms both in developed nations and in parts of the developing areas made it increasingly attractive to locate capital-intensive processing and manufacturing operations in the Third World, even under conditions of a relative abundance of labor. The growth of manufacturing industries had the effect in many African nations of increasing the demand for skilled, or at least semi-skilled, factory operatives, rather than unskilled labor, and of creating a category of employers who had greater interest in the stabilization of labor. This was especially the case where on-the-job training was a necessity and a company expense. At the same time, modernized firms were more willing to pay the associated higher wages, since labor costs were a smaller proportion of total costs. The presence of such new enterprises often increased the pressure on older or locally owned firms to invest likewise in mechanization to cut labor costs.[1]

Migrants, protest and the future

The outcome for workers of these changes in the conditions of capital accumulation depended, however, on the total balance of political–economic forces in the social formation: on industrial structure, on class relations and on the expression of these in state policy. Though there are variations from area to area, one broad contrast stands out; that between East and West Africa, where wages rose and stabilization and skill levels for many African workers increased, and South Africa, where the changes were in the direction of preserving and intensifying the migrant system.

Kenya offers an example of particularly striking changes in employer and government policy, resulting in a decline in short-term labor circulation for many, though by no means all, workers. Full-time workers in the 'formal' (large enterprise) sector are now only migrant in the sense that they usually maintain social ties and some partly developed land holdings in the rural areas, to which they retire after a lifetime of full-time wage earning. Faced with a shortage of skilled labor and rising wages as a result of post War labor militancy, beginning with the Mombasa general strike of 1947, both private industrial and government employers attempted to increase efficiency through training schemes, incentive systems, increased supervision and mechanization, combined with a reduction in the numbers hired. Labor shortages and worker demands reached a crisis point during the Mau Mau rebellion of 1952–5, leading both government and industrial employers to move toward a policy of higher wages and labor stabilization. The turning-point came with the influential Carpenter Committee Report of 1954, which proposed the abolition of the 'bachelor minimum' wage. It argued that the low output and the inefficiency of African labor, long cited as the reasons for low wages, were actually due to the low wages themselves, which inhibited the acquiring of skills. The Report therefore urged more efforts in the direction of labor management and training, and economy in the use of labor. As a result, the adult and youth statutory minimum wages were substantially enhanced, which set the stage for a general rise in wages throughout the economy. The rise in formal-sector real wage rates over the next twenty years was spectacular, only ending in 1972 as a result of growing inflation. Major employers such as the railway, and most particularly the docking industry, continued to substitute capital for labor and to intensify supervision and training, while new foreign-owned firms which arrived tended to be capital-intensive from the beginning. Average skill levels in the formal-sector work force increased, but the corollary of all this seeming progress was an enormous rise in urban unemployment and underemployment and the burgeoning of a low-income 'informal sector'.[2]

Similar dynamics can be seen in West Africa, particularly in certain industries. In Ghana, the colonial government began to grant wage increases during World War II in response to unrest, and between 1940 and 1947 wages in the gold-mines, for example, increased by 30–44%. Labor stabilization in the mines had also increased during the War, and there was a decline in the proportion of migrants from the northern territories and from external groups, such as the Mossi of Upper Volta. The additional pressure of these changes on production costs led mine-owners to institute new 'scientific management' techniques in the attempt to raise productivity. As a result of mechanization, increased supervision, generous bonus schemes and efforts to increase the skill levels of workers, productivity did indeed increase, but so did union power and worker militancy. Wages, therefore, remained high.[3]

In Nigeria too, real wages rose through the 1950s and 1960s, though not nearly as much as they did in Kenya or Uganda, partly because of the government's stated policy goal of wage restraint.[4] A lively debate took place among academic observers as to the causes of this rise, but it seems

Migrants, protest and the future

clear that newly formed industrial unions had some impact on the outcome,[5] not through the agency of Anglo-Saxon style collective bargaining but through the political transmission of wage demands to government commissions and tribunals. But, as in Kenya, the numerous firms which produced either for consumer markets in developed nations or, more commonly, for a growing local urban consumer market (products such as cigarettes, beer, processed foods, cosmetics) could easily offset wage increases by raising prices, since the market was expanding in part because of these very wage increases. The growth of these firms made for a context in which wages could rise.[6]

In both East and West Africa the gap widened between an organized or 'formal' sector of full-time, unionized wage earners working for large firms, and the unorganized 'informal' sector, of part-time and self-employed workers and small firms. In the formal sector even unskilled workers experienced wage increases, because industrial unions incorporated them as members and exerted pressure for general wage increases. Low wages, migrancy, and unemployment, on the other hand, became phenomena of the informal sector. Today, casual and migrant workers are in a much weaker position than they were in the colonial era, both numerically and politically. The situation of the Lagos dock workers described in Chapter 5 well illustrates this point.

Neither blaming unions, as some observers tended to do, nor referring to wages as an autonomously rising factor devoid of institutional context, as neoclassical economists were wont to do, provided an adequate explanation of this transformation. Rather, the combination of large foreign-owned firms 'able to pay', weakened colonial regimes (and later fledgling African governments anxious to keep popular support) and newly powerful African unions and militant workers together resulted in a political–economic context in which wages could rise in the post-War and immediate post-independence years. The net result was a marked reduction in the frequency of short-term migrancy among workers in the 'formal' sector.

These changes in the labor market do not mean that oscillatory migration has decreased in eastern, western and central Africa; only that unskilled migrants today are much less likely to find a paying job. They must more often fall back on small-scale self-employment, or, if they do find employment, it is likely to be part-time, daily-paid or casual work, with little opportunity for advancement. Increasingly, only those migrants with a secondary school education can achieve full-time urban employment. At the same time, population growth, land shortage, growing stratification and the vagaries of cash-crop production in the rural areas mean that migrants continue to stream to African cities and work sites, swelling the ranks of the unemployed and underemployed.

A contrasting trajectory of change has been characteristic of South Africa, where a differering complex of forces has led to the solidification and preservation of low-wage migrancy. Within the pattern of overall growth in the South African economy since the 1930s, the manufacturing sector has grown the fastest, but agricultural production and mining have also continued to flourish. White agriculture has benefited from export markets in Europe, and mining was boosted by the new goldfields which entered production in the late 1940s, by the sustained high price of gold and by the development of mineral resources other than gold, such as iron, copper, platinum, zinc and nickel. Both foreign and local capital are involved in mining and manufacturing, local English and Afrikaaner entrepreneurs appearing to hold their own against foreign competition in many sectors.

The rise of secondary industry here, as elsewhere, did generate pressure for change in the organization of production. Especially in the post-War years there was a need for cost-reducing rationalization to ensure competitiveness against imports. The overall trend in this sector was to dissolve the craft skills, the monopoly of which was the material basis of the privileged position of the white working class. Manufacturers attempted to substitute much cheaper semi-skilled machine operatives who could be recruited from the ranks of black unskilled workers. But this industry was only one element within the powerful capitalist class as a whole.[7]

The new labor needs of industry on the one hand and the coinciding problem of the deterioration of African agriculture in the reserves on the other posed a crisis for the South African migrant-labor system, as did the same contradictions in Kenya. The question was sharply posed in the political arena in South Africa in the 1940s. In broad terms there were two options, the first being to allow the rapidly growing migration of blacks to urban areas to continue, and to grant more Africans permanent residence rights outside the reserves. As it did elsewhere, this policy would probably mean rising wages and increased government expenditure on urban housing and welfare, but it would suit the needs of the manufacturing industries, as would such other changes as removal or raising of job color bars and coopted black trade unions. But the predictable result, the concentration of the majority of the black population in industrial centers such as Durban, Witwatersrand, Capetown and Port Elizabeth, posed enormous and unacceptable political risks for whites. Had the 'liberal' advocates of these policies triumphed, those who believed that industrial development would inevitably undermine racial segregation and white rule would surely have seen their prophecy come to pass.

The second option called for the entrenchment of migrancy, its enforcement and even underwriting by the state and its extension to secondary industry. This was the policy which triumphed with the accession to power of the Nationalist Party in 1948. Africans were not to be permitted to gain residential rights in cities. The provisions of Section 10 of the Black (Urban Areas) Consolidation Act of 1945 as amended provided that no African could remain for more than 72 hours in a 'prescribed' area unless he or she had resided there continuously since birth; had worked there continuously for one employer for ten years; had resided there continuously and legally for fifteen years subject to certain other conditions; was a close dependent relative of, and ordinarily co-resident with, an African who qualified under the foregoing provisions; or had been granted special permission to be in the area. All urban areas were eventually 'prescribed' under the terms of this legislation. All Africans over 16 in South Africa were required to carry a comprehensive reference book, and these influx control measures were applied to women as well as men. During the 1950s the Nationalist government ruthlessly implemented these and other measures designed to make Africans redundant in South Africa in any capacity other than as migrant laborers. Labor bureaus, at which all work-seekers had to register, were established in the reserve areas. Black trade unions continued to be illegal, and black workers were not incorporated into any industrial relations machinery. Urban influx control meant that the widespread proletarianization of Africans in the reserves would not result in the buildup of an urban working class, but rather in an impoverished working class artificially confined to the rural areas.

Industrial decentralization was conceived as a second prong of this strategy, through the 'border industries' program or, as in the case of mining, allowing industrial development in the reserves themselves. To decrease the possible incompatibility between the migrant system and the needs of secondary industry, workers would be encouraged or allowed to take renewable contracts of up to one year, and to decrease absences to only a few weeks' vacation at home. Gradually, the South African government has been drawn into limited programs to encourage agricultural development in the reserves, although this was not originally foreseen because of the ideologically based claim that the reserves were in fact providing a reasonable income to African workers.

In the 1960s, the organic composition of South African capital continued to increase, leading to a rapid rise in the relative surplus population. This structural contradiction gave increased urgency to a new wave of apartheid initiatives, the creation of formally independent bantustans. This strategy divides the population into citizens of South Africa and 'foreigners' with limited rights of entry. This political division does not yet conform to the actual distribution of the population or division of function in the working class, since large numbers of those 'defined out' continue to enter illegally and to form part of the work force, but the stage has been set for the increasing exclusion of 'foreigners' from the labor force.

In the 1960s migrants from newly independent Botswana, Lesotho and Swaziland began to be distinguished from the rest of the work force. Border control posts were established and travel documents required; and, except in mining and agriculture, foreigners were prohibited from taking jobs in South Africa unless the employer could demonstrate that no suitable local labor was available. No foreigners could qualify to remain in urban areas, or indeed in the country, after the expiry of their contracts. Under regulations introduced in 1968 similar restrictions were applied to bantustan residents within South Africa. They were allowed to take work only on the basis of contracts not exceeding one year, at the end of which the worker had to return to his home labor bureau and re-register. Some workers might be granted permission to remain with the same employer without physically returning, but still an entirely new contract was deemed to be in force, and therefore workers recruited under this system could never qualify to live permanently in urban or white areas under the provisions of the Urban Areas Act. Nor could their families ever accompany them while they were away on work contracts.

During the 1970s even the mining industry began to internalize its labor recruitment. As the price of gold rose, beginning in 1972, wages in the industry rose, effectively competing with wages in manufacturing for the first time and therefore attracting sufficient numbers of black South Africans. The independence of Mozambique under the socialist FRELIMO government, and political events in other black-ruled supply countries, provided further reason for the industry to attempt to reduce its dependence on foreign supplies. Colin Murray points out that, whereas in December 1973 'foreign' Africans from Lesotho, Botswana, Swaziland, Mozambique, Zimbabwe and other areas constituted 80% of the black labor force on the mines affiliated to the South African Chamber of Mines, by December 1978 'foreigners' were only 45%, the majority now being black South Africans. It has been estimated that by the year 2000 there will be a 50% reduction in the numbers of Basotho miners.[8] For residents of the bantustans, opportunities in mining increased during the 1970s, but whether this will continue to be the case as the bantustans become independent remains to be seen.

By the late 1970s the first of the bantustans were granted their nominal 'independence'; Transkei in 1976, Bophuthatswana in 1977 and Venda in 1979. In conceding 'independence' to these territories, South Africa has a number of aims. Politically the aim is to forestall and fragment African nationalism, deflecting it from the central goal of majority rule. Part and parcel of this strategy is the nurturing of a collaborative black petty-bourgeoisie and bureaucratic class in the bantustans which will man the surrogate governmental institutions.

The basic economic aim is the continuance of migrant labor. Formal independence transfers much of the cost of shoring up failing agricultural economies to the 'citizens' themselves, or possibly to international donors. As Roger Southall has put it, the Transkei and other bantustans now serve 'ever more explicitly as reservoirs of surplus population, their function being to regulate black wage levels in the metropolitan centers of industry'.[9] Unrest arising from this system can possibly be deflected from South Africa to the bantustan governments. If there should be a move toward higher wages in some sectors of the South African economy, blacks legally resident there could benefit while low-wage migrancy could be confined to 'foreigners' in other sectors.

Thus, throughout the last four decades, South Africa has sought to reverse the 'normal' pattern of capitalist development, in which proletarianized work-seekers migrate more or less permanently to slums on the fringes of industrial areas. In South Africa the reserve army is confined to the rural areas and brought to industrial centers only on short-term contracts according to the needs of capital. Although, as in other parts of Africa, migrancy in South Africa was originally state-induced, today it has to be seen as *state-enforced*. Apartheid policies have functioned as extra-economic measures to hold back the tide of permanent townward migration. The system works because black African workers have developed high levels of skill, experience and dependability *in spite of* their migrancy.

Yet the contradictions in this strategy are inescapable. The bantustans are not in fact economically viable as independent nations. The population now greatly exceeds the carrying capacity of the land, and wage incomes are critical to survival. In the Transkei, for example, some 83% of the region's male labor force was employed as migrant contract labor outside the region or within it. About 60% of all rural households are never able to produce sufficient to feed themselves from their land, even in a good year, and so are fundamentally dependent on the *continued* sale of labor power, not just its intermittent sale. Thus, they must be considered fully proletarianized, if they have access to employment, or else as part of the reserve army of the unemployed.[10] One of the most pervasive features of all bantustans is the high level of unemployment; the other is poverty. These regions have become classic cases of rural underdevelopment, a situation which will lead to increasing pressure to migrate permanently to South Africa and to obtain longer-term jobs with higher wages. Confrontations with the South African state and with employers are inevitable.

Already massive illegal shanty towns are springing up and have been forcibly destroyed. And workers who are enforcedly migrant have been at the forefront of some of the recent labor upheavals in South Africa. In the late 1970s and early 1980s, world economic recession and inflation have led to a squeeze on workers. There have been waves of struggle – strikes, riots and guerilla violence – in industry and in the community, in 1972–4, 1976 as a result of Soweto, 1979–81 and 1984. Whatever the future course of events in South Africa, whether it is armed struggle, a negotiated transfer of power to blacks or both, genuine social change can come about only through the abolition of the migrant-labor system.

MIGRANTS AND CLASS CONSCIOUSNESS

Throughout this examination of migrancy in Africa, we have sought to determine what responses migrant workers have had to their dual role as peasants and as workers. To appreciate fully the impact of migrancy on worker consciousness, we must look not at the contemporary situations of declining migrancy in the full-time labor force in eastern, western and central Africa, or at the deep proletarianization and enforced rural residency in South Africa, but rather at the history of worker action as it developed throughout Africa before World War II. This historical or developmental approach most clearly reveals the organic relations between migrancy and labor action.

We have seen that migrant labor is a distinct form of labor use congruent with labor-intensive, low-wage, low-skill production. The individual migrant is partly involved in two different modes of production. It follows that migrants are in a particular class position, different from that of fully proletarianized workers. Migrants are a class, in the minimal sense of occupying a definable place in the structure of production. We have seen that they have also at times acted as a class in the larger sense – that of engaging in individual and collective actions aimed at furthering their class interests. Their strategies of class action are particular to their migrant situation, and tend to be distinct from those of more fully proletarianized workers.

Until the 1970s, the literature on migrant labor in Africa not only rejected the relevance of class analysis, but also routinely underplayed the potential of migrant workers for labor protest or class action. Recently, however, new evidence on migrant-worker consciousness, together with a widened conception of what constitutes class action or worker resistance, have led to a reassessment of early formulations. Drawing on this new research, the preceding chapters of this book amply demonstrate that migrants often have a well-developed 'worker consciousness', expressed in patterns of market intelligence, labor mobility, informal protest in day-to-day work life and even militant strike actions. These forms of consciousness can persist despite, or perhaps because of, highly coercive labor-control institutions such as forced recruitment and compound housing.

As capitalism developed in Africa, many societies were initially forced to participate in wage labor. In these cases, where peasant production flourished or was considered satisfactory, the struggle *not* to become a worker became the central dynamic of labor protest. In some cases, such as that of the Giriama in Kenya or that of the Baule in the Ivory Coast, whole societies rebelled at the imposition of colonial rule and labor recruitment. Among individuals, avoidance of forced recruitment and desertion after recruitment were widespread. Bribery of chiefs, hiding in the bush and temporary migration across borders were other tactics. All these efforts bespoke a desire to remain outside the wage system, not to enter it at all.

Throughout the era of widespread migrancy, of part-proletarianization, labor supply was never an abstract, autonomous economic force; it was an arena of struggle between employers and potential workers. Its uncertainty and short-falls were a barometer of African unwillingness to submit to wage exploitation at all, so long as the rural economy provided another option. To work or not to work was a key strategy of self-protection by potential migrants. As some wage work became necessary, often a compromise was chosen: seasonal work, which allowed the rhythm of the agricultural cycle to dictate the length and timing of wage work.

The change from escaping the wage system to various tactics of survival within it is a major one in the evolution of labor protest. It took place in Africa as a result of the increasing debilitation of the peasant economy. Within the wage system, the migrant's chief weapon was market mobility. Not surprisingly, this mobility was the very thing that recruiting systems, long contracts, criminal penalties for 'desertion', pass laws and confining compound systems were designed to curtail. Despite such efforts, desertion from employment was high, now undertaken not with the aim of returning to rural life, but of moving toward higher-paid work elsewhere in a regional market, such as successive jobs that would support a worker in his migration through central Africa toward the Rand. Another manifestation of mobility was the avoidance of 'bad' employers. Mines, farms or companies which paid lower wages, had high accident and sickness rates, or reputations for harsh management suffered shortages throughout the era of labor migration, sometimes having to turn to the state for provision of forced labor. The benefits of mobility were also seen in the tendency for more experienced and proletarianized migrants to avoid recruitment organizations and long contracts in favor of independent migration and shorter contracts. Whereas some employment areas such as the Copperbelt made a fairly quick transition away from recruitment systems toward exclusively 'voluntary' labor, almost the opposite trend took place in South Africa; over the years it became less and less easy to enter South Africa in this way. The large 1971 strike of Ovambo workers in Namibia was an attempt to achieve precisely this freedom from repressive recruitment systems.

Mobility from job to job could be an effective strategy only in a general context of labor shortage or of shortage of particular types of skilled labor. Mobility back to the rural area could be effective only so long as the peasant economy could provide adequate support. Therefore, as proletarianization and labor supply increased, it became more and more necessary to turn to labor action on the job. Instead of escaping from adverse employment situations, it became necessary to negotiate. Almost all the early strikes by migrant workers took place in contexts in which, for one reason or another, it was nearly impossible for them to leave. Forced laborers, compound residents and migrants from especially long distances were in this situation.

Strikes by migrants can be effective if they take place

during periods of labor shortage, and if subsistence from the rural areas makes possible a longer strike. Compound systems were probably effective in controlling desertion and theft, but they seem actually to have promoted coordinated strike action. But several factors undermine migrants' ability to mount successful strike actions: skill levels tend to be low, so that workers are easily replaced; ethnic divisions more easily undermine the unity of large strikes, since the work force is recruited from many different areas; (ethnic ties can also promote collective action among a homogeneous work force, however, and such actions, though sometimes making use of traditional cultural idioms such as language and clothing, are in no way traditional in their leadership or aims); and, finally, though migrancy does not inhibit strike actions or individual forms of on-the-job protest, it does seem to render more difficult the formation of ongoing formal organizations of workers. When workers' associations and unions emerged in Africa, they did so among the more stabilized, higher-skilled workers first, then spread gradually through the work force. And many, though not all, of the large and successful strike actions have involved both migrant and stabilized workers, with the latter providing leadership and organizational support.

This brief review of the evolution of labor protest among migrant workers demonstrates the pervasive influence of the rural economy on the character of resistance. Where the rural economy provides an alternative to wage labor, workers are always apt to leave to return to it. Where the rural economy is undermined, labor-market mobility is still a main strategy of migrant workers in their attempts to move from job to job. Where the rural sector is severely undermined, strikes and other on-the-job actions become more prevalent. In the extreme case of widespread proletarianization, unemployment may be so high that all labor action is undermined, and the individualized struggle just to get access to the labor market may take precedence.

Migrants, protest and the future

Today, migrants no longer benefit from strategies of market mobility such as 'desertion', because there is no longer a general situation of labor shortage. In eastern, western and central Africa, where the context is one of high unemployment, migrant and casual workers must adopt the strategies of the organized, full-time labor force, coordinating strike actions with them if they are to succeed. In South Africa, the context of over-supply and repression of formal organizations also makes it difficult for strike action to succeed. But the homogeneity of certain work-place factors, such as barracks accommodation, influx control, job color bars and low wages, makes it possible for many migrants to continue to struggle collectively to better their situation.

NOTES

1 MIGRATION AND DEVELOPMENT

1 Robert E. Johnson, *Peasant and Proletarian: The Working Class of Moscow in the Late Nineteenth Century* (New Brunswick, N J: Rutgers University Press, 1979), pp. 12–13.
2 Jean Chesneaux, *The Chinese Labor Movement, 1919–1927* (Stanford, Calif.: Stanford University Press, 1968) pp. 50–64; T. Wright, '"A Method of Evading Management" – Contract Labor in Chinese Coal Mines before 1937', *Comparative Studies in Society and History*, 23:4 (October, 1981), 656–78.
3 Joan Nelson, 'Temporary Versus Permanent Cityward Migration: Causes and Consequences', *Economic Development and Cultural Change*, 24 (1976), 721–57.
4 Audrey I. Richards, *Economic Development and Tribal Change: A Study of Immigrant Labour in Buganda* (London: Oxford University Press, 1973) (first published, 1954); Polly Hill, *Migrant Cocoa Farmers in Southern Ghana* (Cambridge: Cambridge University Press, 1963); Sara Berry, *Cocoa, Custom and Socio-Economic Change in Rural Western Nigeria* (London: Oxford University Press, 1975). In some cases kin groups migrate with a mixture of motives, ready to accept wage work, but also looking to establish themselves more or less permanently as independent cash crop growers. For the suggestion that one such group is a 'permanent hybrid of peasant and proletarian', see Edward A. Alpers, '"To Seek a Better Life": The Implications of Migration from Mozambique to Tanganyika for Class Formation and Political Behavior', *Canadian Journal of African Studies* 18, 2 (1984), pp. 367–88.
5 Ray Bromley and C. Gerry, 'Who are the Casual Poor?', in R.

Bromley and C. Gerry, eds., *Casual Work and Poverty in Third World Cities* (New York: John Wiley & Sons, 1979), pp. 3–27.

6 David Parkin, 'Introduction', in D. Parkin, ed., *Town and Country in Central and Eastern Africa* (London: Oxford University Press, for the International African Institute, 1975), pp. 9–10.

7 Samir Amin, 'Introduction', in S. Amin, ed., *Modern Migrations in Western Africa* (London: Oxford University Press, for the International African Institute, 1974), p. 92.

8 J. R. Harris and M. P. Todaro, 'Migration, Unemployment and Development: A Two-Sector Analysis', *American Economic Review*, 60:1 (March, 1970), 126–42; John Harris, 'A Conceptual Framework for the Study of Migration in Botswana', Boston University African Studies Center, Working Paper No. 42, 1981; Michael P. Todaro, *Internal Migration in Developing Countries*, (Geneva: International Labor Office, 1976).

9 Harold Wolpe, 'Capitalism and Cheap Labour-Power in South Africa: From Segregation to Apartheid', *Economy and Society*, 1:4 (1972), 425–56; Martin Legassick, 'South Africa: Capital Accumulation and Violence', *Economy and Society*, 3:3 (1974), 253–91.

10 Patrick Harries, 'Kinship, Ideology and the Nature of Pre-Colonial Labour Migration: Labour Migration from the Delagoa Bay Hinterland to South Africa, up to 1895', in S. Marks and R. Rathbone, eds., *Industrialisation and Social Change in South Africa* (London: Longman, 1982), pp. 142–3. But after the state-supported monopsony was established African wages in South Africa did not again reach their 1896 peak until 1945: F. A. Wilson, *Labour in the South African Gold Mines, 1911–1969*, (Cambridge: Cambridge University Press, 1972), pp. 4, 45–6, 53, 55, 141.

11 This point has been made by, among others, Michael Burawoy, 'The Functions and Reproduction of Migrant Labor: Comparative Material from Southern Africa and the United States', *American Journal of Sociology*, 81:5 (1975/6), 1050–87.

12 From a large literature on labor systems, see E. LaClau, 'Feudalism and Capitalism in Latin America', *New Left Review* 67 (May–June, 1971); E. Genovese, *The Political Economy of Slavery* (New York: Vintage, 1965); M. L. Morris, 'The Development of Capitalism in South African Agriculture: Class Struggles in the Countryside', *Economy and Society*, 5:3 (1976), 292–343. Whether and in what sense

these systems are 'capitalist' has been the subject of protracted debate. See especially LaClau, 'Feudalism'; J. Banaji, 'Modes of Production in a Materialist Conception of History', *Capital and Class*, 3 (1977), 1–44; W. Roseberry, 'Peasants as Proletarians', *Critique of Anthropology*, 3:11 (1978), 3–18. H. Bernstein, 'Notes on Capital and Peasantry', *Review of African Political Economy*, 10 (1977), pp. 60–73. Minimally, they are capitalist in that they produce for a world market and that many of the inputs or means of production are controlled by capital. But they have seemingly non-capitalist modes of labor mobilization.

13 Shula Marks and Richard Rathbone, 'Introduction', in Marks and Rathbone, eds., *Industrialisation and Social Change*, p. 15.

14 Charles van Onselen, *Chibaro: African Mine Labour in Southern Rhodesia, 1900–1933* (London: Pluto Press, 1976), p. 76–7.

15 Charles Perrings, 'Review Article: The Southern African Gold Mining Industry', *Journal of African History*, 18 (1977), 129–35.

16 David Beach, 'The Shona Economy: Branches of Production', in R. Palmer and N. Parsons, eds., *Roots of Rural Poverty in Central and Southern Africa* (Berkeley: University of California Press, 1977), pp. 37–65.

17 Sharon Stichter, *Migrant Labour in Kenya: Capitalism and African Response, 1895–1975* (London: Longman, 1982), p. 16.

18 C. van Onselen, 'Reactions to Rinderpest in Southern Africa, 1896–97', *Journal of African History*, 23 (1972), 473–88.

19 Ester Boserup, *Women's Role in Economic Development* (New York: St Martin's Press, 1970), Chap. 1.

20 E. S. Atieno Odhiambo, 'The Movement of Ideas: A Case Study of Intellectual Responses to Colonialism among the Liganua Peasants', in B. A. Ogot, ed., *Hadith 6* (Nairobi: East African Literature Bureau, 1976), pp. 165–85; or as in Amin's report of the Zarma (see p. 5 above).

21 G. Clarence-Smith and R. Moorsom, 'Underdevelopment and Class Formation in Ovamboland, 1844–1917', in Palmer and Parsons, eds., *Roots*, p. 107.

22 In the case of migrant farm-workers, another point of similarity with pre-colonial times may be noted. In both African and white-settler cash-crop areas, workers often 'bound' themselves and their families under the personal protection of the farmer in a manner reminiscent

of pre-colonial fealty relationships. For example, see J. Kimble, 'Labour Migration in Basutoland, c. 1870–1885', in Marks and Rathbone, eds., *Industrialisation*, p. 120.
23 Pierre-Philippe Rey, 'Sur l'Articulation des modes de production', in P-P. Rey, *Les Alliances de classes* (Paris: Maspero, 1973).
24 Marks and Rathbone, 'Introduction', in *Industrialisation*, p. 20.
25 Harries, 'Kinship, Ideology', p. 144.
26 See the discussion in Van Onselen, *Chibaro*, pp. 87–91, of the movement of Shangaan workers into Southern Rhodesia and then back to South Africa. In 1902 no less than 55% of black Southern Rhodesian miners were Shangaans.
27 Sherilyn Young, 'Fertility and Famine: Women's Agricultural History in Southern Mozambique', in Palmer and Parsons, eds., *Roots*, p. 72–3.
28 This interpretation is derived from Harries.
29 Young, 'Fertility and Famine', p. 73.
30 A. Rita-Ferreira, 'Labour Emigration among the Mozambique Thonga: Comments on a study by Marvin Harris', *Africa*, 30 (1960), 143.
31 This account follows Peter Delius, 'Migrant Labour and the Pedi, 1840–80', in S. Marks and A. Atmore, eds., *Economy and Society in Pre-Industrial South Africa* (London: Longman, 1980), pp. 293–312.
32 Kimble, 'Labour Migration', p. 135.
33 This account draws on W. G. Clarence-Smith, *Slaves, Peasants and Capitalists in Southern Angola, 1840–1926* (Cambridge: Cambridge University Press, 1979), and on Clarence-Smith and Moorsom, 'Underdevelopment and Class Formation'.
34 Clarence-Smith and Moorsom, 'Underdevelopment and Class Formation', p. 107.
35 Bill Freund, *Capital and Labour in the Nigerian Tin Mines*, Ibadan History Series (London: Longman, 1981), pp. 47, 51.
36 Stichter, *Migrant Labour*, pp. 4–5; Freund, *Capital and Labour*, pp. 47, 52.
37 Timothy C. Weiskel, 'Labor in the Emergent Periphery: From Slavery to Migrant Labor among the Baule Peoples, 1880–1925', in W. Goldfrank, ed., *The World System of Capitalism* (Beverly Hills, Calif.: Sage Publications, 1979), pp. 207–31.
38 Clarence-Smith, *Slaves*, p. 32.

39 R. L. Tignor, *The Colonial Transformation of Kenya: Kamba, Kikuyu and Masai from 1900 to 1939* (Princeton, NJ: Princeton University Press, 1976).
40 One exception among the Maasai was women, who found a flourishing market for their sexual services in nearby Nairobi.
41 Martin Chanock, 'Agricultural Change and Continuity in Malawi', in Palmer and Parsons, eds., *Roots*, pp. 396–409.
42 F. E. Sanderson, 'The Development of Labour Migration from Nyasaland, 1891–1914', *Journal of African History*, 2 (1961), 259–71.
43 Van Onselen, *Chibaro*, pp. 94–5.

2 MIGRANTS AND THE RURAL ECONOMY

1 Godfrey Wilson, *Essay on the Economics of Detribalization in Northern Rhodesia*, Rhodes-Livingstone Papers, Nos. 6 and 5 (Cape Town: Oxford University Press, 1941–2).
2 Isaac Schapera, *Migrant Labour and Tribal Life: A Study of Conditions in the Bechuanaland Protectorate* (London: Oxford University Press, 1947).
3 P. H. Gulliver, *Labour Migration in a Rural Economy: A Study of the Ngoni and Ndendeuli of Southern Tanganyika*, East African Studies, No. 6 (Kampala, 1955).
4 Audrey I. Richards, *Land, Labour and Diet in Northern Rhodesia* (London: Oxford University Press, 1939).
5 Margaret Read, 'Migrant Labour in Africa and its Effects on Tribal Life', *International Labour Review*, 45 (1942), 605–31.
6 M. Wilson, S. Kaplan, T. Maki, and E. M. Walton, *Keiskammahoek Rural Survey, Vol. III: Social Structure* (Pietermaritzburg: Shuter & Shuter, 1952).
7 Max Gluckman, *Essays on Lozi Land and Royal Property*, Rhodes-Livingstone Papers, No. 10 (Cape Town: Oxford University Press, 1943); *idem*, 'The Lozi of Barotseland in North-Western Rhodesia', in E. Colson and M. Gluckman, eds., *Seven Tribes of British Central Africa* (London: Oxford University Press, 1951).
8 William Watson, *Tribal Cohesion in a Money Economy: A Study of the Mambwe People of Northern Rhodesia* (Manchester: Manchester University Press, 1958).

9 J. Van Velson, 'Labour Migration as a Positive Factor in the Continuity of Tonga Tribal Society', *Economic Development and Cultural Change*, 8 (1960), 265–78.
10 Walter Elkan, *Migrants and Proletarians* (London: Oxford University Press, 1960).
11 Colin Bundy, *The Rise and Fall of the South African Peasantry* (London: Heinemann, 1979).
12 Robin Palmer, 'The Agricultural History of Rhodesia', in Palmer and Parsons, eds., *Roots*, pp. 221–54. This volume argued the underdevelopment case for the whole of central and southern Africa.
13 E. A. Brett, *Colonialism and Underdevelopment in East Africa* (London: Heinemann, 1973); see also S. Stichter, *Migrant Labour*, pp. 69–80.
14 Terence Ranger, 'Growing from the Roots: Reflections on Peasant Research in Central and Southern Africa', *Journal of Southern African Studies*, 5:1 (October, 1978), 99–117 (p. 99).
15 Bundy, *Rise and Fall*, p. 243.
16 Robin Cohen, 'From Peasants to Workers in Africa', in P. C. W. Gutkind and Immanuel Wallerstein, eds., *The Political Economy of Contemporary Africa* (Beverly Hills, Calif.: Sage Publications, 1976), pp. 155–68 (p. 161).
17 For example, Elizabeth Colson, 'Migration in Africa: Trends and Possibilities', in F. Lorimer and M. Karp, eds., *Population in Africa* (Boston, Mass.: Boston University Press, 1960), pp. 60–7; Watson, *Tribal Cohesion*, p. 110; Read, 'Migrant Labour', p. 622.
18 Watson, *Tribal Cohesion*, p. 111; M. Gluckman, 'Forward', in *Ibid.*, p. vii.
19 The Ndebele, however, were not solely plunderers and cattle-keepers, but also had quite a diversified agriculture as well as a flourishing regional trade: Palmer, 'Agricultural History', p. 224–5; G. Arrighi, 'Labour Supplies in Historical Perspective: A Study of the Proletarianization of the African Peasantry in Rhodesia', *Journal of Development Studies*, 6:3 (April, 1970), 197–234, especially pp. 202–3, 228–9. See Chapter I above for the origins of wage labor among the Shona.
20 Watson, *Tribal Cohesion*, p. 107
21 *Ibid.*, pp. 106–11.
22 *Ibid.*, pp.112–16. This argument was also advanced by Read, who contrasted the patrilineal Ngoni with the matrilineal Chewa.

23 Van Velson, 'Labour Migration'.
24 Watson, *Tribal Cohesion*, pp. 66–7.
25 Elliott P. Skinner, 'Labour Migration and its Relationship to Socio-Cultural Change in Mossi Society', *Africa*, 4 (1960) 375–99; *idem*, 'Labor Migration among the Mossi of the Upper Volta', in Hilda Kuper, ed., *Urbanization and Migration in West Africa* (Berkeley: University of California Press, 1965), pp. 60–84. The following account is drawn from these two sources.
26 This social structure, Skinner argues, made it easier for the French to impose forced labor in the 1920s, since the Mossi had a tradition of rendering corvée labor to their chiefs.
27 See Chapter 4 below.
28 S. Coulibaly, J. Gregory, et V. Piché, *Les Migrations voltaiques, Tome I: Importance et ambivalence de la migration voltaique* (Ottawa: Centre de Recherches pour le Développement International, 1980), République de Haute-Volta, Institut National de la Statistique et de la Démographie, p. 39, 43.
29 William Beinart, 'Labour Migrancy and Rural Production: Pondoland, c. 1900–1950', in P. Mayer, ed., *Black Villagers in an Industrial Society* (Cape Town: Oxford University Press, 1980), pp. 81–108; *idem*, 'Production, Labour Migrancy and the Chieftaincy: Aspects of the Political Economy of Pondoland, ca. 1860–1930', Ph.D. thesis, University of London, 1979.
30 Beinart, 'Production', p. 227.
31 Beinart, 'Labour Migrancy', pp. 89, 90.
32 *Ibid.*, p. 98. Beinart advances some of these arguments a bit more tentatively than I have here.
33 Colin Bundy, 'The Transkei Peasantry, c. 1890–1914: "Passing through a Period of Stress"', in Palmer and Parsons, eds., *Roots*, pp. 201–20 (p. 208).
34 Joel W. Gregory and Victor Piché, 'African Population: Reproduction for Whom?', *Daedalus*, 3:2 (Spring, 1982), 179–209, especially pp. 198–9. They draw on the well-known theses of J. Caldwell, *Theory of Fertility Decline* (New York: Academic Press, 1982), and extend his argument to migrant labor. However, historically there have been cases where, because of the high mortality of migrants or their lengthy absence, the spread of venereal disease, or the decline in the rural standard of living, the population in the rural areas has

declined, and there has been a probable fall in the birth-rate: see Harries, 'Kinship, Ideology', p. 155, for the Delagoa Bay area of Mozambique; Bruce Fetter, 'Labor Migration and Infertility in Central Africa: A Regional Approach', paper presented to the Annual Meeting of the African Studies Association, Boston, December, 1983.

35 For example, new research now suggests that birth-rates in Western Europe increased prior to the Industrial Revolution, and that the fastest-growing areas were those where cottage industry flourished and new factory and mining towns sprang up: see Wally Seccombe, 'Marxism and Demography', *New Left Review*, 137 (January–February, 1983), 22–47.

36 Gregory and Piché, 'African Population', p. 200.

37 H. Rempel and R. Lobdell, 'Urban-to-Rural Remittances: Investment in Rural Development or Insurance Premium?', paper presented to the Annual Meeting of the Canadian Association of African Studies, Sherbrooke, Quebec, May, 1977.

38 Harries, 'Kinship, Ideology', p. 153.

39 Colson, 'Migration in Africa'.

40 Michael Cowen, 'Differentiation in a Kenya Location', East African Social Science Research Council conference paper, 1972; M. P. K. Sorrenson, *Land Reform in the Kikuyu Country* (London: Oxford University Press, 1967); Stichter, *Migrant Labour*, pp. 102–4.

41 A case which is similar today, but which evolved from the superimposition of cash-cropping on a labor reserve economy, is that of Inhambane Province in Mozambique, described by Ruth First in *Black Gold: The Mozambican Miner, Proletarian and Peasant*, pp. 123–179. Here the increase in non-forced peasant production of groundnuts, cashews and coconuts in the 1960s coincided with only a small drop in the flow of experienced, long-contract migrants to the South African gold mines. As among the Kikuyu, labor migration today remains a critical income source for the poorer peasants, who supply the most recurrent migration, but is also an important source for all peasants of the cash needed to acquire a wife, agricultural implements such as ploughs, and consumption goods. The poorer districts are similar to Lesotho, described below, in that they show an especially close relationship between migrant wages and social differentiation, the most well-off families being those of boss-boys on the mines. Ruth First believes that only cooperative and collective forms

of development in the peasant economy can provide an alternative to migrant labor in Mozambique as well as avoid the social differentiation brought on by cash cropping for the world market.
42 Jeanne Henn, 'Peasants, Workers, and Capital: The Political Economy of Labor and Incomes in Cameroon', Ph.D. thesis, Harvard University, 1978.
43 Jette Bukh, *The Village Woman in Ghana* (Uppsala: Scandinavian Institute of African Studies, 1979), pp. 33–6, 94.
44 Sara S. Berry, 'Oil and the Disappearing Peasantry: Accumulation, Differentiation and Underdevelopment in Western Nigeria', paper presented to the Boston University Seminar series, October, 1982.
45 Sara S. Berry, 'Work, Migration and Class in Western Nigeria', in F. Cooper, ed., *Struggle for the City* (Beverly Hills, Calif.: Sage Publications, 1983), pp. 247–73, especially p. 261.
46 Colin Murray, *Families Divided: The Impact of Migrant Labour in Lesotho* (Cambridge: Cambridge University Press, 1981).
47 *Ibid.*, p. 153.
48 *Ibid.*, p. 154.
49 *Ibid.*, p. 41.
50 *Ibid.*, pp. 51, 19, 96.
51 *Ibid.*, pp. 76–9.

3 MIGRATION AND THE AFRICAN HOUSEHOLD

1 Claude Meillassoux, *Maidens, Meal, and Money: Capitalism and the Domestic Community* (Cambridge: Cambridge University Press, 1981). Meillassoux's formulation, however, does not actually specify the exploitation of women *via* the transfer of surplus, so that gender exploitation, though it exists, is not class exploitation: see pp. 50–60, 75–81 of *Maidens*, and Maureen Mackintosh, 'Reproduction and Patriarchy: A Critique of Meillassoux, "Femmes, Greniers, et Capitaux"', *Capital and Class*, 2 (1977), 119–27.
2 Pierre-Philippe Rey, 'The Lineage Mode of Production', *Critique of Anthropology*, 3 (Spring, 1975), 27–79.
3 Caldwell, *Theory of Fertility Decline*.
4 Jeanne K. Henn, 'The Material Basis of Sexism: A Mode of Production Analysis', paper presented to the Annual Meeting of the African Studies Association, Boston, November, 1983; Nancy Folbre, 'A

Patriarchal Mode of Production', unpublished manuscript, May, 1984; *idem*, 'Exploitation Comes Home: A Critique of the Marxian Theory of Family Labour', *Cambridge Journal of Economics*, 6 (1982), 317–29.

5 The domestic labor debate is a lengthy and complex one which cannot be adequately dealt with here. Suffice it to say that those who argue for a 'patriarchal mode' maintain: a) that reproductive labor cannot be excluded from the economic base or infrastructure of a mode of production, and that failure to include it was the most serious flaw in the traditional Marxian conception (see Seccombe, 'Marxism and Demography', and Folbre, 'A Patriarchal Mode'; b) that the alleged problem of incommensurability between commodity-producing labor and labor within a non-capitalist mode can be solved through the concept of surplus-labor, opening the way for a theory of articulation (see Henn, 'The Material Basis'; Folbre, 'Exploitation').

6 Henn, 'The Material Basis'. On the elders as an exploiting class, see Rey, 'The Lineage Mode'. For the argument that elders are not a class, since their dominance is temporary, and since there can be no class exploitation in a pre-capitalist society, see Emmanuel Terray, *Marxism and Primitive Societies* (New York: Monthly Review Press, 1972), although Terray has since reversed his position. For a critique of both on the grounds of ignoring the exploitation of women, see Maxine Molyneaux, 'Androcentrism in Marxist Anthropology', *Critique of Anthropology*, 3:9 & 10, (1977), 55–81.

7 Henn, 'Peasants, Workers and Capital', pp. 80–2. Folbre has delineated the ways in which this schematic 'patriarchal mode' could apply to the pre-colonial systems both of the Shona and of the Ndebele of Zimbabwe, also arguing that the structure of this mode placed strict limits on the rate of exploitation: 'Zimbabwe and the Lineage of Patriarchal Capitalism', unpublished manuscript.

8 Lack of space prevents a systematic analysis in this chapter of the effects on household size or on divorce rates.

9 Gluckman, *Essays on Lozi Land*, p. 50.

10 Watson, *Tribal Cohesion*, pp. 42–3.

11 *Ibid.*, pp. 63–5, 70.

12 *Ibid.*, pp. 153–8.

13 Skinner, 'Labour Migration among the Mossi', p. 73.

14 *Ibid.*, pp. 74–5; Watson, *Tribal Cohesion*, pp. 44–6.

15 Skinner. 'Labour Migration among the Mossi', p. 74. One woman threatened to run off with 'any stranger on his way to Kumasi' if her husband did not reform.
16 Coulibaly, Gregory and Piché, *Les Migrations voltaiques*, p. 43; Watson, *Tribal Cohesion*, p. 44. For the threat to elders' power posed by women's migration, see Chapter 6 below.
17 There are very few in-depth accounts of the inpact of labor migration on societies where domestic slavery was common. For a review of the initial effects in one case, see Weiskel, *French Colonial Rule and the Baule Peoples* (Oxford: Clarendon Press, 1980), pp. 235–44.
18 Changes in the sexual division of labor were also noted for the Tsonga of Mozambique, described in Chapter 1. See Young, 'Fertility and Famine'.
19 Stichter, *Migrant Labour*, Table 2.5 and, pp. 55, 99, 105.
20 Margaret Jean Hay, 'Luo Women and Economic Change during the Colonial Period', in Nancy Hafkin and Edna Bay, eds., *Women in Africa: Studies in Social and Economic Change* (Stanford, Calif.: Stanford University Press, 1976), pp. 87–110.
21 Achola O. Pala, 'Women's Access to Land and Their Role in Agriculture and Decision-Making on the Farm: Experiences of the Joluo of Kenya', Institute for Development Studies Discussion Paper No. 263 (Nairobi, 1978).
22 Margaret Jean Hay, 'Women as Owners, Occupants, and Managers of Property in Colonial Western Kenya', in M. Hay and Marcia Wright, eds., *African Women and the Law: Historical Perspectives*, Boston University Papers on Africa, No. 7, 1982, pp. 110–23, especially pp. 112, 117.
23 Jane Guyer, 'The Economic Position of Beti Widows, Past and Present', Boston University African Studies Center, Working Paper No. 22, 1979, pp. 9–11.
24 Pala, 'Women's Access to Land', pp. 10–11.
25 Henn, 'Peasants, Workers and Capital', pp. 80–2, 136–8.
26 *Ibid.*, pp. 263–4.
27 For an illuminating comparison of two contrasting cases, the Yoruba and the Beti, see Jane I. Guyer, 'Food, Cocoa, and the Division of Labour by Sex in Two West African Societies', *Comparative Studies in Society and History*, 22:3 (July, 1980), 355–73. For further information on the Yoruba, see Sara S. Berry, *Cocoa, Custom and*

Socio-Economic Change in Rural Western Nigeria (London: Oxford University Press, 1975); Niara Sudarkasa, *Where Women Work: A Study of Yoruba Women in the Market-place and in the Home* (Ann Arbor: University of Michigan, 1973).

28 Guyer, 'Food, Cocoa, and the Division of Labour'; Jane Guyer, 'Women in the Rural Economy: Contemporary Variations', in M. Hay and S. Stichter, eds., *African Women South of the Sahara* (London: Longman, 1984), pp. 19–32.

29 Sharon Stichter, 'Women and the Labor Force in Kenya, 1895–1964', *Rural Africana*, 29 (1975–6), 45–67, and additional sources cited there.

30 Susan Abbott, 'Full-Time Farmers and Weekend Wives: An Analysis of Altering Conjugal Roles', *Journal of Marriage and the Family*, 38:1 (February, 1976), 165–74.

31 Greet Kershaw, 'The Changing Roles of Men and Women in the Kikuyu Family by Socio-Economic Status', *Rural Africana*, 29 (1975–6), 173–94, especially pp. 186–92.

32 The following account is drawn from Bukh, *Village Woman*.

33 *Ibid.*, pp. 84–8.

34 See Chapter 2 above.

35 Guyer, 'Food, Cocoa and the Division of Labour', pp. 361–2. The following account is derived from this source.

36 Murray, *Families Divided*, p. 41.

37 *Ibid.*, pp. 54, 155.

38 Jef Leeuwenberg, *The Transkei: A Study in Economic Regression* (London: Africa Publications Trust, 1977), pp. 2–8.

39 Bukh, *Village Woman*, p. 43.

40 Martha Mueller, 'Women and Men, Power and Powerlessness in Lesotho', in Wellesley Editorial Committee, ed., *Women and National Development: The Complexities of Change* (Chicago, Ill.: University of Chicago Press, 1977), pp. 154–66.

41 Murray, *Families Divided*, pp. 158–60.

42 Colin Murray, 'High Bridewealth, Migrant Labour and the Position of Women in Lesotho', *Journal of African Law*, 21:1 (1977), 79–96.

43 *Ibid.*, p. 88.

44 *Ibid.*, pp. 92–4.

45 Murray, *Families Divided*, p.166.

46 Although some would argue for more terminological and statistical

precision, the terms 'rate' and 'incidence' are used here in the manner proposed by J. Clyde Mitchell, 'The Causes of Labour Migration', *Bulletin of the Inter-African Labour Institute*, 6:1 (1959), 12–47; Reprinted in J. Middleton, ed., *Black Africa* (London: Macmillan, 1970).

47 Henn, 'Peasants, Workers, and Capital', pp. 262–97, 352–3.
48 Wolpe, 'Capitalism and Cheap Labour-Power'; Carmen Diana Deere, 'Rural Women's Subsistence Production in the Capitalist Periphery', *Review of Radical Political Economics*, 8:1 (Spring, 1976), 9–17.
49 Caldwell, *Theory of Fertility Decline*.
50 Seccombe, 'Marxism and Demography'.

4 ENTERING AND LEAVING THE WORK FORCE

1 Paul Lubeck, 'Class Formation at the Periphery: Class Consciousness and Islamic Nationalism among Nigerian Workers', in R. L. Simpson and I. Simpson, eds., *Research in the Sociology of Work*, Vol. 1 (Greenwich, Conn.: JAI Press, Inc., 1981), pp. 37–70; *idem*, 'The Leburori within the Urban Talakawa' unpublished manuscript.
2 The Baule of the Ivory Coast, for example, resisted French conquest in a series of revolts which turned directly on the issues of labor: French demands for porters and other tribute labor and, most fundamentally, their policy of freeing the domestic slaves: see Timothy C. Weiskel, 'Labor in the Emergent Periphery'; *idem*, *French Colonial Rule and the Baule*.
3 Richard Waller, 'The Masai and the British, 1895–1905: The Origins of an Alliance', *Journal of African History*, 17:4 (1976), 529–53.
4 Roger G. Thomas, 'Forced Labour in British West Africa: The Case of the Northern Territories of the Gold Coast, 1906–1927', *Journal of African History*, 14:1 (1973), 79–103.
5 Michael Mason, 'Working on the Railway: Forced Labor in Northern Nigeria, 1907–1912', in R. Cohen, J. Copans, and P. C. W. Gutkind, eds., *African Labor History* (Beverly Hills, Calif.: Sage Publications, 1978), pp. 56–79; quotation from p. 65.
6 Dennis D. Cordell and Joel W. Gregory, 'Labour Reservoirs and Population: French Colonial Strategies in Koudougou, Upper Volta, 1914–1939', *Journal of African History*, 23:2 (1982), 205–24.

7 A. I. Asiwaju, 'Migrations as Revolt; The Example of the Ivory Coast and the Upper Volta before 1945', *Journal of African History*, 17:4 (1976), 577–94. See also the description of the Mossi in Chapter 2 above.
8 Myron Echenberg, 'Paying the Blood Tax; Military Conscription in French West Africa, 1914–1929', *Canadian Journal of African Studies*, 9:2 (1975), 171–92; Myron Echenberg, 'Military Migrations in French West Africa, 1900–1945', *Canadian Jounal of African Studies*, 14:3 (1980); Myron Echenberg and Jean Filipovich, 'African Forced Labour in the *Office du Niger* Development Project, 1925–1950', paper presented to the CAAS Conference, Nova Scotia, May 9–12, 1984.
9 Jeanne Penvenne, 'Forced Labor and the Origin of an African Working Class: Lourenço Marques, 1870–1962,' Boston University African Studies Center, Working Paper No. 13, 1979.
10 Marvin Harris, 'Labour Migration among the Mozambique Thonga: Cultural and Political Factors', *Africa*, 29:1 (1959), 50–64.
11 Penvenne, 'Forced Labor', p. 8.
12 Stichter, *Migrant Labour*, pp. 51–2.
13 Penvenne, 'Forced Labour', p. 5. The continuing significance of *chibalo* up to the mid 1960s is noted in First, *Black Gold*; see especially the interview with José Kumbe, pp. 42–3.
14 Freund, *Capital and Labour*, pp. 51, 74.
15 Thomas, 'Forced Labour', p. 83.
16 Mason, 'Working on the Railway', pp. 67–75.
17 In the early years all these centers of prospecting and development had managed to attract a 'voluntary' labor supply, the reasons for which were discussed in Chapter 1. Such workers came largely from Mozambique, South Africa and Nyasaland (Malawi) and were soon quite skilled and experienced. What the mines really needed, and could not get, was large quantities of cheap unskilled labor.
18 In theory, but often not in practice, recruiting was also expected to smooth out the seasonal fluctuations in supply which resulted from the strength of the peasant economy, as well as to make possible longer-term projections of labor costs.
19 Wilson, *Labour in the South African Gold Mines*, p. 4; D. J. N. DeNoon, 'The Transvaal Labour Crisis, 1901–6', *Journal of African History*, 8:3 (1967), 481–94.
20 Van Onselen, *Chibaro*, pp. 25, 75; Arrighi, 'Labor Supplies'. For the

continuing importance of officially recruited low-wage contract workers in Rhodesia from 1946 to 1971 see D. Clarke, *Contract Workers and Underdevelopment in Rhodesia* (Gwelo: Mambo Press, 1974).

21 Van Onselen, *Chibaro*, pp. 25, 114, 116.
22 Charles Perrings, *Black Mineworkers in Central Africa: Industrial Strategies and the Evolution of an African Proletariat in the Copperbelt, 1911–41* (London: Heinemann, 1979), pp. 56, 42.
23 Perrings, *Black Mineworkers*, p. 56; Charles Perrings, '"Good Lawyers but Poor Workers": Recruited Angolan Labour in the Copper Mines of Katanga, 1917–1921', *Journal of African History*, 18:2 (1977), 237–59.
24 Perrings, *Black Mineworkers*, pp. 148–51, 154, 165.
25 Van Onselen, *Chibaro*, p. 104.
26 Perrings, *Black Mineworkers*, p. 20.
27 Van Onselen, *Chibaro*, pp. 95–6.
28 See maps in Perrings, *Black Mineworkers*: Fig. 3 (p. 149) and Fig. 2 (p. 72). The Mambwe, Bemba and Ngoni are discussed in Chapter 2.
29 See map in Perrings, *Black Mineworkers*: Fig. 5 (p. 191).
30 Wilson, *Labour in the South African Gold Mines*, p. 69 and map (p. x).
31 Perrings, *Black Mineworkers*, pp. 92, 95.
32 Van Onselen, *Chibaro*, pp. 99, 104.
33 *Ibid.*, pp. 104–5.
34 Perrings, *Black Mineworkers*, pp. 22, 152.
35 Van Onselen, *Chibaro*, p. 105.
36 For examples in Kenya, see Stichter, *Migrant Labour*, p. 38; for Angola, see Perrings, *Black Mineworkers*, p. 152.
37 Perrings, *Black Mineworkers*, p. 181.
38 Van Onselen, *Chibaro*, p. 106; for background, see Perrings, *Black Mineworkers*, pp. 15–18.
39 Van Onselen, *Chibaro*, p. 107.
40 *Ibid.*, p. 110.
41 Jane L. Parpart, *Labor and Capital on the African Copperbelt* (Philadelphia, Pa: Temple University Press, 1983), p. 31–2.
42 Perrings, *Black Mineworkers*, Fig. 5 (p. 191).
43 Stichter, *Migrant Labour*, pp. 81–3.
44 Perrings, *Black Mineworkers*, p. 155.
45 Perrings, 'Good Lawyers', p. 256.

46 Perrings, *Black Mineworkers*, p. 182. As late as the 1950s Clarke reports desertion rates of 17.4% in 1957 and 16.6% in 1958 among Rhodesian Native Labor Supply Commission contract workers from Nyasaland and elsewhere. See Clarke, *Contract Workers*, pp. 55–6.
47 Quoted in Van Onselen, *Chibaro*, p. 109; Perrings makes a similar point about recruited Angolan workers in 'Good Lawyers', p. 252.
48 William Beinart, 'Joyini Inkomo: Cattle Advances and the Origins of Migrancy from Pondoland', *Journal of Southern African Studies*, 15:2 (April, 1979), 199–219.
49 *Ibid.*, p. 215.
50 Perrings, *Black Mineworkers*, pp. 154–5.
51 *Ibid.*, pp. 182–5.
52 Richard Moorsom, 'Underdevelopment, Contract Labour and Worker Consciousness in Namibia, 1915–72', *Journal of Southern African Studies*, 4:1 (October, 1977), 52–87. The following account draws largely from this source. The origins of wage labor among the Ovambo are described in Chapter I above.
53 L. Douwes Dekker, D. Hemson, J. S. Kane-Berman, J. Lever and L. Schlemmer, 'Case Studies in African Labour Action in South Africa and Namibia', in R. Sandbrook and R. Cohen, eds., *The Development of an African Working Class* (London: Longman, 1975) pp. 226–32.
54 Quoted in Moorsom, 'Underdevelopment', p. 86.

5 MIGRANTS AT THE WORK PLACE

1 For a very useful discussion of these forms and their interrelation, see Robin Cohen, 'Resistance and Hidden Forms of Consciousness Amongst African Workers', *Review of African Political Economy*, 19 (September–December, 1980), 8–22.
2 The most significant differences, we have argued, are not between the migrant and the non-migrant workers, but between the partly and fully proletarianized. For example, most contemporary workers in South Africa are still migrant, but they are highly proletarianized.
3 For a general review of worker consciousness in Africa, see Richard Sandbrook, 'Worker Consciousness and Populist Protest in Tropical Africa', in R. Simpson and I. Simpson, eds., *Research in the Sociology of Work*, (Greenwich, Conn.: JAI Press Inc., 1981), pp. 1–36.
4 Stichter, *Migrant Labour*, p. 137.

5 The basic sources for these strikes are, for *Durban*: David Hemson, 'Dock Workers, Labour Circulation, and Class Struggles in Durban, 1940–59', *Journal of Southern African Studies*, 4:1 (October, 1977), 88–124; for *Mombasa*: A. Clayton and D. C. Savage, *Government and Labour in Kenya, 1895–1963* (London: Frank Cass, 1974); F. Cooper, 'Urban Disorder and the Transformation of Work: The Docks of Mombasa, 1934–1955', Boston University, African Studies Center Seminar Paper, April, 1982; and S. Stichter, *Migrant Labour*; for *Dar-es-Salaam*: John Iliffe, 'A History of the Dockworkers of Dar-es-Salaam', *Tanzania Notes and Records*, 71 (1970); for *Zanzibar City*: Anthony Clayton, *The 1948 Zanzibar General Strike*, Scandinavian Institute of African Studies, Research Report No. 32 (Uppsala, 1976).

6 There were also a number of early strikes by West African dock workers, notably two in Lagos in 1919 and 1920, both involving casual workers, as well as the participation of harbor and wharf workers in the famous five-month 1947 railway strike in French West Africa. See Arnold Hughes and Robin Cohen, 'An Emerging Nigerian Working Class: The Lagos Experience, 1897–1939', and J. Suret-Canale, 'The French West African Railway Workers' Strike, 1947–1948', both in P. C. W. Gutkind, R. Cohen and J. Copans, eds., *African Labor History* (Beverly Hills, Calif.: Sage Publications, 1978).

7 Hemson, 'Dock Workers', p. 92.

8 Clayton, *The 1948 Strike*, pp. 26–7; Hemson, p. 111.

9 Hemson, 'Dock Workers', p. 123.

10 *Ibid.*, p. 96.

11 Cooper, 'Urban Disorder', pp. 2, 20.

12 See the further discussion in Stichter, *Migrant Labour*, pp. 111, 166.

13 *Ibid.*, p. 138.

14 Hemson, 'Dock Workers', p. 122.

15 Peter Waterman, *Division and Unity amongst Nigerian Workers: Lagos Port Unionism, 1940's–60's*, Institute of Social Studies Research Report Series, No. 11 (The Hague: Institute of Social Studies, 1982), pp. 55–7; *idem*, 'Consciousness, Organisation and Action amongst Lagos Portworkers', *Review of African Political Economy*, 13 (May–August, 1978), 47–62, especially p. 48.

16 Waterman, *Division and Unity*, pp. 106–7.

17 *Ibid.*, pp. 168–76.

18 Van Onselen, *Chibaro*, pp. 128–30.
19 *Ibid.*, pp. 131–3; D. J. N. DeNoon, 'The Transvaal Labour Crisis'.
20 Van Onselen, *Chibaro*, pp. 133–4.
21 Perrings, *Black Mineworkers*, p. 110–11.
22 Jane L. Parpart, *Labor and Capital on the African Copperbelt*, pp. 38–46.
23 Van Onselen, *Chibaro*, pp. 136–53. For descriptions of life and work in South African mines today, from the workers' point of view, see First, *Black Gold, passim*, especially pp. 96–107 and photos; L. Callinicos, *A People's History of South Africa, Vol. I: Gold and Workers*; and recent issues of the *South African Labour Bulletin*. For Tswana workers' views of the mines, ranging from 'inhuman' and 'horrible' (older workers, less dependent on the mines) to 'it makes us men' and 'the money is a joy' (younger, poorer men), see Hoyt Alverson, *Mind in the Heart of Darkness* (New Haven, Conn.: Yale University Press, 1978), pp. 216–36.
24 Robert J. Gordon, *Mines, Masters and Migrants* (Johannesburg: Ravan Press, 1977).
25 Van Onselen, *Chibaro*, pp. 239–44; P. Richardson and J. Van-Helten, 'Labour in the South African Gold Mining Industry, 1886–1914', in Marks and Rathbone, eds., *Industrialisation and Social Change*, pp. 77–98.
26 Sean Moroney, 'Mine Worker Protest on the Witwatersrand: 1901–1912', in Eddie Webster, ed., *Essays in Southern African Labour History* (Johannesburg: Ravan Press, 1978), pp. 32–46.
27 Peter Warwick, 'Black Industrial Protest on the Witwatersrand, 1901–1902', in Webster, ed., *Essays*, pp. 20–31.
28 Philip Bonner, 'The 1920 Black Mineworkers' Strike: A Preliminary Account', In Belinda Bozzoli, ed., *Labour, Townships and Protest: Studies in the Social History of the Witwatersrand* (Johannesburg, Ravan Press, 1979), pp. 273–97.
29 Van Onselen, *Chibaro*, pp. 218–26.
30 I. R. Phimister, 'The Shamva Mine Strike of 1927: An Emerging African Proletariat', *Rhodesian History*, 2 (1971), 65–88.
31 Parpart, *Labor and Capital*, pp. 54–5, 62, 71.
32 Charles Perrings, 'Consciousness, Conflict and Proletarianization: An Assessment of the 1935 Mineworkers' Strike on the Northern Rhodesian Copperbelt', *Journal of Southern African Studies*, 4:1 (October, 1977), 31–51 (pp. 36–7).

33 Parpart, *Labor and Capital*, p. 160.
34 Perrings, 'Consciousness, Conflict'.
35 Jeanne Penvenne, 'Worker Intelligence Networks in Lourenço Marques, Mozambique, 1900–1962', paper presented at the Annual Meeting of the African Studies Association, Los Angeles, November, 1979.
36 Lucy Jayne Kamau Botscharow, 'Domestic Service in Nairobi, Kenya', unpublished manuscript, 1976.
37 Penvenne, 'Worker Intelligence'.
38 Charles van Onselen, 'The Witches of Suburbia: Domestic Service on the Witwatersrand, 1890–1914', in C. van Onselen, ed., *Studies in the Social and Economic History of the Witwatersrand, 1886–1914*, Vol. 2: *New Nineveh* (Johannesburg: Ravan Press, 1982); Stichter, *Migrant Labour*, pp. 121, 171.
39 Stichter, *Migrant Labour*, p. 171.
40 Van Onselen, 'Witches', p. 59.

6 WOMEN AS MIGRANTS AND WORKERS

1 Ester Boserup, *Women's Role in Economic Development* (New York: St Martin's Press, 1970), p. 190.
2 Deborah Bryceson, 'The Proletarianization of Women in Tanzania', *Review of African Political Economy*, 17 (January–April, 1980), 4–27.
3 Iris Berger, 'Sources of Class Consciousness: South African Women in Recent Labor Struggles', *International Journal of African Historical Studies*, 16:1 (1983), 49–66; quotation from p. 50.
4 Karl Marx, *Capital*, trans. E. and C. Paul (New York: International Publishers, 1929), p. 791.
5 Claire Robertson and Iris Berger, eds., 'Introduction', *Women and Class in Africa* (New York: Africana Publishing Corporation, forthcoming).
6 Marx, *Capital*, p. 792.
7 For an analysis of the parallels and differences between the situation of employed women and male migrant workers, see Veronica Beechey, 'Female Wage Labour in Capitalist Production', *Capital and Class*, 3, 1977, pp. 45–66.
8 In general, more theoretical work needs to be done on the implica-

tions of the sex division of domestic and reproductive work for male, as well as female, labor-force participation.
9 R. H. Sabot, *Economic Development and Urban Migration: Tanzania, 1900–1971* (Oxford: Clarendon Press, 1979), pp. 89–98. See also Nwanganga Shields, 'Women in the Urban Labor Markets of Africa: The Case of Tanzania', World Bank Staff Working Paper, No. 380, April, 1980, pp. 23–6.
10 Christine Obbo, *African Women: Their Struggle for Economic Independence* (London: Zed Press, 1980), Table 7 (p. 71).
11 Niara Sudarkasa, 'Women and Migration in Contemporary West Africa', in Wellesley Editorial Committee, eds., *Women and National Development* (Chicago: University of Chicago Press, 1977), pp. 178–89. This picture of independent female migrants may be altered as more recent data become available.
12 Obbo, *African Women*, Table 8 (p. 76).
13 Skinner, 'Labor Migration among the Mossi', pp. 66, 74.
14 Obbo, *African Women*, p. 80.
15 *Ibid.*, p. 79.
16 For example, Sabot, *Economic Development*, p. 95; Sudarkasa, 'Women and Migration', p. 185.
17 Obbo, *African Women*, p. 72. See Chapter 3 for the Mossi and the Mambwe.
18 Obbo, *African Women*, pp. 72–3. A similar point is made by Sudarkasa for wives of Yoruba migrants to Ghana ('Women and Migration', p. 182).
19 Bukh, *Village Woman*, p. 36.
20 Maud Muntemba, 'Thwarted Development: A Case Study of Economic Change in the Kabwe Rural District of Zambia, 1902–70', in Palmer and Parsons, eds., *Roots*, pp. 345–64, especially pp. 346, 354–5, 359–60. The 1969 census revealed 52,496 men in this district and only 50,611 women – an unusual situation for any part of rural Africa.
21 Barbara B. Brown, 'Women, Migrant Labor and Social Change in Botswana', Boston University African Studies Center, Working Paper No. 41, 1980, p. 3.
22 Julia Wells, 'Passes and Bypasses: Freedom of Movement for African Women Under the Urban Areas Act of South Africa', in Hay and Wright, eds., *African Women and the Law*, pp. 126–50.

23 *Ibid.*, pp. 126–7, drawing on B. A. Pauw, *Xhosa in Town: The Second Generation* (Cape Town, 1963).
24 George Chauncey, Jr, 'The Locus of Reproduction: Women's Labour in the Zambian Copperbelt, 1927–1953', *Journal of Southern African Studies*, 7:2 (April, 1981), 135–64, especially pp. 154–6.
25 Jane L. Parpart, 'Class and Gender on the Copperbelt: Women in the Northern Rhodesian Copper Mines, 1926–1964', in Robertson and Berger, eds., *Women and Class in Africa*.
26 The following account is from Chauncey, 'Locus of Reproduction', 157–60.
27 Quoted *Ibid.*, p. 159.
28 This account follows Wells, 'Passes and Bypasses', pp. 129–50.
29 See Hilda Bernstein, *For Their Triumphs and for Their Tears: Women in Apartheid South Africa* (London: International Defence and Aid Fund, 1977).
30 Olubanke Akerele, *Women Workers in Ghana, Kenya, Zambia* (Addis Ababa: African Training and Research Centre for Women, 1979), Table 6. All such official figures undoubtedly underestimate the number of women in urban domestic service and in wage work in the informal sector.
31 Amelia Mariotti, 'The Incorporation of African Women into Wage Employment in South Africa, 1920–1970', Ph.D. thesis, University of Connecticut at Storrs, 1979, p. 186.
32 For a fuller discussion, see Sharon Stichter, 'Some Selected Statistics on African Women', in Hay and Stichter, eds., *African Women South of the Sahara*, pp. 188–94.
33 Lourdes Beneria, 'Conceptualizing the Labor Force: The Underestimation of Women's Economic Activities', in Nici Nelson, ed., *African Women in the Development Process* (London: Frank Cass, 1981), pp. 10–28.
34 International Labor Organization, *Labour Force Estimates and Projections, 1950–2000*, 2nd edn (Geneva, 1977), Table 2.
35 Akerele, *Women Workers*, Table VIII (p. 39).
36 Mariotti, 'Incorporation of African Women', p. 286.
37 Akerele, *Women Workers*, p. 41. In the sample of Ghanaian factory workers in Accra interviewed by Margaret Peil in 1966, 12% were women, most of whom were in semi-skilled positions such as seamstresses. They were young and likely to be un-married, and there

was no evidence that they were less stable on the job than men: M. Peil, *The Ghanaian Factory Worker: Industrial Man in Africa* (Cambridge: Cambridge University Press, 1972), pp. 24, 46, 102.
38 African Training and Research Centre for Women, *Women Textile Workers in Ethiopia* (Addis Ababa: United Nations Economic Commission for Africa, 1979).
39 Mariotti, 'Incorporation of African Women', pp. 188–9.
40 *Ibid.*, Table 42 (p. 223).
41 Berger, 'Sources of Class Consciousness', p. 53, n. 11.
42 Barbara Rogers, *Divide and Rule: South Africa's Bantustans* (London: International Defence and Aid, 1976), p. 76.
43 Sharon Stichter, 'The Division of Household Labor and Decision-Making among Middle-Income Families in Nairobi', unpublished manuscript, 1983.
44 Mariotti, 'Incorporation of African Women', pp. 210–11, 286, Table 31.
45 Stichter, 'Some Selected Statistics', Table 7 (p. 192).
46 Republic of Kenya, Central Bureau of Statistics, *Women in Kenya* (Nairobi, 1978), pp. 43–6.
47 Ilsa Schuster, 'Female White Collar Workers: A Case Study of Successful Development in Lusaka, Zambia', Women in Development Working Paper No. 29, (Ann Arbor: Michigan State University, 1983).
48 Akerele, *Women Workers*, p. 35.
49 Schuster, 'Female White Collar Workers', p. 2.
50 *Ibid.*, pp. 5, 20. Schuster emphasized the more disturbing aspects of their lives, the instability of marital and romantic relationships, in *New Women of Lusaka* (Palo Alto, Calif.: Mayfield Publishing Company, 1979).
51 Stichter, 'Some Selected Statistics', Table 7 (p. 192).
52 Charles van Onselen, 'Worker Consciousness in Black Miners: Southern Rhodesia, 1900–1920', *Journal of African History*, 14:2 (1973), 237–55.
53 Parpart, 'Class and Gender on the Copperbelt', p. 4. The following section draws on this source.
54 Sembene Ousmane, *God's Bits of Wood* (London: Heinemann, 1970).
55 Schuster, *New Women*, pp. 91–103.
56 Helen I. Safa, 'Class Consciousness among Working Class Women in

Latin America: A Case Study in Puerto Rico', in R. Cohen, P. Gutkind and P. Brazier, eds., *Peasants and Proletarians: The Struggles of Third World Workers* (New York: Monthly Review Press, 1979).

57 Jaclyn Cock, *Maids and Madams: A Study in the Politics of Exploitation* (Johannesburg: Ravan Press, 1980); quotation from pp. 7–8. About half of these domestic workers were migrants, sending money back to families in the bantustans; the rest were more or less permanently urbanized.

58 *Ibid.*, pp. 83–4.

59 *Ibid.*, pp. 66–7.

60 *Ibid.*, pp. 106, 115–18.

61 *Ibid.*, pp. 49, 53, 84. Other studies have found up to 80% of female domestic workers were the sole support of their families (*ibid.*, p. 312).

62 *Ibid.*, pp. 51–2, 113–15.

63 *Ibid.*, p. 105.

64 *Ibid.*, p. 53.

65 Berger, 'Sources of Class Consciousness', p. 58.

66 See, for example, Jean Westmore and Pat Townsend, 'The African Women Workers in the Textile Industry in Durban', *South African Labour Bulletin*, 2:4 (1975), 21–30.

67 Nancy Van Vuuren, *Women Against Apartheid: The Fight for Freedom in South Africa* (Palo Alto: R and E Associates, 1979), p. 96.

68 Dekker *et al.*, 'Case Studies in African Labour Action', pp. 216–17.

69 D. du Toit, *Capital and Labour in South Africa: Class Struggle in the 1970's* (London: Routledge and Kegan Paul, 1981).

70 Berger, 'Sources of Class Consciousness', pp. 59–61.

71 Westmore and Townsend, 'Women Workers in the Textile Industry', p. 26.

72 Berger, 'Sources of Class Consciousness', p. 62; drawing from Natal Labour Research Committee, 'Control Over a Workforce – the Frame Case', *South African Labour Bulletin*, 6:5 (December, 1980).

7 MIGRANTS, PROTEST AND THE FUTURE

1 Ernest Mandel, *Late Capitalism* (London: New Left Books, 1975); Giovanni Arrighi, 'International Corporations, Labour Aristocracies, and Economic Development in Tropical Africa', in R. I. Rhodes,

ed., *Imperialism and Under-development* (New York: Monthly Review Press, 1970), pp. 220–67.
2 Stichter, *Migrant Labour*, pp. 133–49; Alice Amsden, *International Firms and Labour in Kenya: 1945–1970* (London: Frank Cass, 1972).
3 Jeff Crisp, 'Productivity and Protest: Scientific Management in the Ghanaian Gold Mines, 1947–1956', in F. Cooper, ed., *Struggle for the City*, pp. 91–130.
4 This point was made by John Weeks, 'Wage Policy and the Colonial Legacy', *Journal of Modern African Studies*, 9:3 (October, 1971), 361–88.
5 See Peter Kilby, 'Industrial Relations and Wage Determinations: Failure of the Anglo-Saxon Model', *Journal of Developing Areas*, 1 (July, 1967), 489–520; W. M. Warren, 'Urban Real Wages and the Nigerian Trade Union Movement, 1939–60', *Economic Development and Cultural Change*, 15:1 (October, 1966), 21–36. For opposing views, see Elliot J. Berg, 'Urban Real Wages and the Nigerian Trade Union Movement, 1939–60: A Comment', *Ibid.*, 17:4 (July, 1969), 604–17; John F. Weeks, 'A Comment on Peter Kilby: Industrial Relations and Wage Determination', *Journal of Developing Areas*, 3:1 (October, 1968), 7–17.
6 Kilby, 'Industrial Relations', pp. 500–1.
7 Legassick, 'South Africa: Capital Accumulation and Violence'. The account which follows draws mainly from this source, from Wolpe, 'Capitalism and Cheap Labour-Power in South Africa', and from M. Legassick and H. Wolpe, 'The Bantustans and Capital Accumulation in South Africa', *Review of African Political Economy*, 7 (September–December, 1976), 87–107.
8 Murray, *Families Divided*, pp. 29–31.
9 Roger Southall, *South Africa's Transkei: The Political Economy of an "Independent" Bantustan* (London: Heinemann, 1982), p. 39.
10 Duncan Innes and Dan O'Meara, 'Class Formation and Ideology: The Transkei Region', *Review of African Political Economy*, 7 (September–December, 1976), 71.

INDEX

alcohol, 37, 120, 150, 152, 164, 167, 171, 183
Amin, Samir, 5
Angola, 12, 19–23, 103, 106–7, 111, 159
Asia, 1, 25, 144, 145

bantustans, 55, 158, 161, 174, 187, 188–90, 218 n. 57
Barotse, 30, 35
Baule, 23, 192, 208 n. 2
Beinart, William, 43, 113
Belgian Congo: see Zaire
Bemba, 30, 33, 35, 36–7, 106, 137, 138, 155
Berger, Iris, 146
Berry, Sara, 52, 53
Beti, 61, 68, 69–70, 74, 76–77, 206 n. 27
Blomfontein, 157
Bophuthatswana, 161–2, 188
border industries, 161–2, 174, 186
Botswana, 30, 90, 106–7, 153–4, 159, 160, 187, 188, 213 n. 23
Bourse du Travail du Katanga (BTK), 102–8, 111, 115
bridewealth, 13, 15–6, 61, 63, 64, 69, 80–1; brideprice, 34, 47, 113, 154
Bryceson, Deborah, 146
Buganda, 3; see also Uganda
Bukh, Jette, 51, 78

'cadets': see 'young men'
Caldwell, John, 60, 85, 87, 202 n. 34
Cameroon, 33, 50–1, 61, 68, 69–70, 76–77, 84, 159, 160

capital, 2, 179–182, 184, 187, 189, 198 n. 12
capitalist mode of production: see mode of production, capitalist
capitalization, level of, 8, 9, 94
cash crops, 33, 48–9, 50–2, 56, 63, 69–77, 153, 184, 198 n. 22, 203 n. 41; cocoa, 3, 33, 40, 50–3, 68–70, 74–7, 153; coffee, 3, 33, 40, 50; cotton, 3, 39, 42; effect on fertility, 85–6; maize, 43–4
cassava, 38, 67, 75, 76
Chauncey, George, 155
chiefs: buying land, 49; role in female migration, 156–7; role in labor migration, 12–22, 41; role in labor recruitment, 40, 94, 96, 99, 100–1, 202 n. 26
China, 1
Chopi, 14–15
Cock, Jaclyn, 169, 170, 172, 173
cocoa: see cash crops, cocoa
coffee: see cash crops, coffee
Cohen, Robin, 32
Colson, Elizabeth, 48
communication, among workers, 120, 123, 125, 137, 139, 143, 174
compounds, 8, 26, 117, 118, 123, 125, 129–35, 136–7, 138, 143, 150, 153, 156, 157, 165–8, 174, 192, 194
contracts: see labor contracting
Cooper, Fred, 126
Copperbelt: see mines, copper
copper mines: see mines, copper
cotton: see cash crops, cotton

221

Dakar, 97
Dar-es-Salaam, 124, 125
deferred payment systems, 13, 107, 111, 113, 114, 115
desertion from employment, 8, 26, 88, 96–7, 99, 100–1, 104, 109, 111, 114–15, 116, 120–1, 130, 131, 134, 135, 165, 192–3, 194, 195, 210–11 n. 46
desertion of women by men, 147, 148, 151
divorce, 75, 78, 80, 147, 148, 151, 168, 171, 205 n. 8
dock workers and docking industry, 121, 122–9, 142–3, 182, 195, 212 n. 6
domestic workers, 55, 79, 82, 118, 121, 138–41, 142, 150, 154, 161, 162–3, 168–74
drought, 10, 15, 20, 56
Durban, 124, 125, 126, 127, 141, 158, 174, 176, 177, 185

education: importance of, 45–6, 87, 89, 184; investment in, 50, 51, 52, 73, 75, 86, 172; women and, 149, 150, 151, 152, 154, 162, 163, 165
elders, 10, 12–22, 24, 47, 59, 60–81, 82–5, 86, 94, 148, 155–7, 167, 205 n. 6
Elkan, Walter, 31
Ethiopia, 160
Europe, Western, 25, 86
European settlers: see white settlers
Ewe, 51–2, 74–5, 76, 77, 78

female-headed households: see women
First, Ruth, 203–4 n. 41
Folbre, Nancy, 60
forced labor, 4, 7–8, 10, 14, 24–8, 40–1, 93–101, 108–9, 193, 202 n. 26, 209 n. 13; resistance to, 41, 89, 192
French West Africa, 96, 97, 99, 166, 212, n. 6

Ghana, 3, 33, 40, 41, 42, 50–2, 74–5, 84, 95, 100, 144, 153, 159, 160, 164, 182, 216–7 n. 37
Giriama, 192
Gluckman, Max, 30, 34, 35, 63
gold mines: see mines, gold
Gordon, Robert, 133
Gregory, Joel, 45
Guinea–Bissau, 159
Gulliver, P. H., 30
Guyer, Jane, 68
Gwari, 100–1

Harries, Patrick, 47
Harris, Marvin, 98
Hausa, 22, 23
Hay, Margaret Jean, 66, 67
Hemson, David, 125, 126
Henn, Jeanne, 60, 69, 84

Ivory Coast, 23, 40, 41, 42, 159, 192, 208 n. 2

Johannesburg, 44, 79, 81, 140, 141, 174, 176

Kamba, 10
Kampala, 150–2, 168
Katanga, 8, 94, 101, 102–3, 104, 105, 106, 107, 108, 109, 110, 111, 115, 131, 138
Kenya, 9, 10, 12, 24, 28, 32, 33, 35, 39, 47, 48–50, 71–4, 95, 99, 110, 124–7, 139, 140, 141, 144, 159, 160, 163, 181–2, 183, 185, 192
Kershaw, Greet, 72, 73
Kibachia, Chege, 125
Kikuyu, 33, 35, 48–50, 71–4, 79, 126

labor coercion: see forced labor
labor contracting, 1, 96, 128–9, 130, 186–7, 188, 192, 193; advances, 107, 112–15; contract details, 13, 55, 91, 102, 103, 107, 108, 110, 111, 115, 117, 126

Index

labor protest, 5, 91, 92, 97–8, 99, 101, 116–19, 120–1, 124–7, 134–8, 139, 140, 141, 146, 164–78, 179–81, 190, 191–5
labor recruiting, 8, 16, 26, 89, 94–5, 98–9, 101–19, 192–3, 209–10 n. 20
Lagos, 128–9, 195, 212 n. 6
Lamba, 156
Latin America, 1, 144
Legassick, Martin, 7
Lesotho, 44, 54–7, 77–81, 83, 90, 153, 159, 160, 187, 188; Sotho kingdom, 17, 18–19, 21, 63
lineage mode of production: *see* mode of production, lineage
Lourenço Marques: *see* Maputo
Lozi, 63
Lubeck, Paul, 89
Luo, 12, 35, 39, 66–8, 126
Lusaka, 163–4
Luyia, 39, 126

Maasai, 24, 35, 47, 95, 200 n. 40
Malawi, 26–7, 28, 30, 31, 106–7, 108, 174
Mali, 97, 159
Mambwe, 31, 33, 35, 36–8, 39, 41, 43, 54, 64–5, 106
Maputo, 14, 98, 99, 124, 139, 140
Marks, Shula, 9
Marx, Karl, 146, 147, 149
Mason, Michael, 100
matrilineality, 37–8, 59, 146, 153, 201 n. 22
Mauritius, 144
Meillassoux, Claude, 60, 204 n. 1
Mijikenda, 126–7
miners, 3, 22, 121, 122, 123, 129–38, 160
mines and mining industry, 8, 25, 27, 41, 54, 55, 80, 101, 103, 104, 115, 121, 129–38, 142–3, 155–7, 184, 186, 187, 188, 193; copper, 4, 21, 30, 101, 110, 131–2, 136–8, 155–6, 165–8, 193; diamond, 10, 17, 18, 19, 21, 101, 130, 133; gold, 4, 10, 19, 44, 95–6, 100, 101, 102, 105, 130, 134, 182, 184, 188, 203 n. 41, 213 n. 23; tin, 22, 23, 99, 102
mode of production: capitalist, 1, 7, 59, 179; domestic, 59, 60; family, 60; lineage, 60; patriarchal, 60, 62, 81–7, 205 n. 5, 205 n. 7
Mombasa, 123–7
Moorsom, Richard, 119
Morocco, 144
mortality, 45, 132; mortality rates, 40, 87, 96, 97, 106, 134, 202 n. 34
Mossi, 33, 39–42, 43, 54, 64–5, 97, 151, 182
Mozambique, 14, 15, 47, 93–4, 98–9, 104, 106–7, 108, 112, 139, 140, 188, 203–4 n. 41
Mpondo, 43–4, 113–15
Muntemba, Maud, 153
Murray, Colin, 54, 55, 57, 77, 78, 79, 80, 83, 188
Mvubelo, Lucy, 175

Nairobi, 139, 140–1
Namibia, 21, 106–7, 116–19, 133, 193
Nandi, 35
Ndebele, 35, 111, 201 n. 19, 205 n. 7
Ngoni, 27, 30, 35, 106, 156
Nguni, 14–15
Nigeria, 3, 22, 23, 33, 50, 51, 52–3, 70–1, 84, 89, 96, 99, 100–1, 128–9, 159, 182–3
northeastern Rhodesia: *see* Zambia
Northern Rhodesia: *see* Zambia
Northern Rhodesia Native Labour Association (NLA), 102, 107
Nupe, 100
Nyasaland: *see* Malawi

Obbo, Christine, 150, 151, 152, 168
Okeyo, Achola Pala, 66, 68
Orange Free State, 157–8
Ovambo, 12, 14, 19–22, 24, 27, 116–19, 193

palm oil, 3
Parkin, David, 5
Parpart, Jane, 137, 165
pass laws, 15, 54, 139, 140, 143, 154, 157, 173–4, 178, 186, 192
pastoralists, 2, 47–8, 59
Pedi, 13, 14, 17–8, 24, 63
Perrings, Charles, 9, 103, 138
Phimister, I. R., 135
Phungula (Zulu), 125, 126
Piché, Victor, 45
polygyny, 60, 148, 151, 154
population growth, 34, 45–6, 66, 82, 85–7, 94, 184, 189, 203 n. 35
Portuguese areas, 9, 14, 19–21, 23, 27, 93–4, 98–9; *see also* Angola, Guinea-Bissau, Mozambique
prostitution, 113, 150, 155, 167, 200 n. 40

race and racial divisions in the work force, 130, 133–4, 137–8, 168–9, 171, 175, 185
railways and railway workers, 10, 21, 41, 94, 96, 97, 100, 101, 104, 110, 121, 122, 124, 166, 182, 212 n. 6
Read, Margaret, 30, 35
religious movements, 120, 136
remittances: *see* wages
reproduction, 58, 61, 80, 85–7, 145, 147–9, 165, 168, 177, 179, 205 n. 5, 215 n. 8
Rey, Pierre-Philippe, 13, 60
Rhodesia: *see* Southern Rhodesia; Zimbabwe
Rhodesian Native Labour Bureau (RNLB), 102–3, 104, 105, 107, 108, 109, 110, 111, 112
Richards, Audrey, 30, 35
rinderpest, 10, 20, 56, 113
Russia, 1, 25
Rwanda, 3, 152

Sabot, R. H., 150
Schapera, Isaac, 30

Schuster, Ilse, 163, 164
seasonal patterns of wage work, 21–2, 39, 40, 41, 44, 54, 66, 91, 115, 117, 192, 209 n. 18
Seccombe, Wally, 85
Shangaans, 14, 199 n. 26
Shona, 10, 35, 111, 205 n. 7
skill divisions in work force, 128, 129, 131, 138, 139
skilled workers, 49, 91–2, 121, 124, 128, 130, 133, 137, 141, 160, 162, 180, 181, 185, 193, 194
Skinner, Elliott, 39, 64, 65
slavery, 8, 9, 147, 148; abolition of, 21, 23, 69, 208 n. 2; forced, contract and other labor as, 96, 98, 108, 118, 172; household slaves, 10, 20, 22–3, 60–3, 147; slave trading, 11, 19–20; as source of wage labor, 22–3, 62–3, 94, 206 n. 17
sleeping sickness, 109
Sotho: *see* Lesotho
South Africa, 2, 8, 9, 14–22, 25, 26, 30, 31, 33, 43–4, 45, 54–6, 63, 83, 89, 98, 99, 101, 102–3, 104, 105, 106, 107, 110, 111, 116, 124, 125, 126, 129, 130, 131, 132, 133, 134–5, 144, 146, 149, 154, 157–8, 159, 160–1, 162, 163, 164, 168–78, 180–1, 184–90, 191, 193, 195, 213 n. 23
Southall, Roger, 189
Southern Rhodesia, 8, 9, 10, 14, 27, 31, 99, 101, 102, 104, 105, 106, 107, 108, 109, 131, 132, 135; *see also* Zimbabwe
strikes, 26, 98, 99, 116–9, 120–1, 123, 124–6, 129, 132, 134–8, 141, 142–3, 149, 164, 165, 166, 174, 175–6, 181, 190, 193–4, 195 212 n. 6
Sudan, 3, 159
Swaziland, 187, 188

Tanzania, 3, 30, 106–7, 124, 125, 126
taxation: by chiefs, 16, 18, 21; by

colonial governments, 19, 25, 26–8, 40, 69, 94, 106, 109, 136, 137
textile and garment factories and workers, 1, 122, 144, 160–1, 169, 174–7
theft, 120, 130, 134, 140, 165, 173, 194
Thuku, Harry, 140
Tonga, 31, 35, 38, 39, 48
trade unions: *see* union formation and trade unions
Transkei, 43, 78, 90, 113–15, 188, 189–90
Tsonga, 14–17, 24, 47, 63, 99, 206 n. 18

Uganda, 3, 31, 95, 150–2, 168, 182
union formation and trade unions, 120, 121, 122, 125, 128–9, 137, 138, 139, 140, 141, 149, 164, 165, 166, 174, 175–6, 177, 178, 182, 183, 186, 194
Upper Volta, 33, 39–42, 97, 151, 182

Van Onselen, Charles, 105, 110, 125, 134, 135, 141, 164
Van Velson, J., 31, 38, 39
Venda, 188

wages, 7–8, 17, 19, 25, 28, 56, 66, 69, 72, 82, 84–5, 89, 91, 93, 98, 101, 102–3, 104, 105, 107, 111, 113, 115, 116, 118, 122, 123, 124, 125, 127, 131, 133, 134, 136, 137, 141, 142, 145, 148, 153, 156, 161, 162, 165, 166, 168, 170, 172, 174, 176, 180–4, 188, 189, 197 n. 10; differentials in work force, 104, 116, 138, 139, 176; disposition of, 4, 148; effect on fertility, 87; remittances, 46, 77, 78–9
Waterman, Peter, 128, 129
Watson, William, 31, 35, 36, 37, 38, 39, 64, 65

white-collar, salaried and professional workers, 49, 50, 51, 53, 73, 87, 91–2, 122, 161, 162–4, 168, 172; clerks, 3, 125, 133, 136
white settlers, 9, 11, 12–13, 24, 25, 26, 27, 48, 56, 121, 160, 198 n. 22; Afrikaaners, 15, 17, 18, 184
widows and widowhood, 61, 68, 78, 147, 150, 151, 153, 154
Wilson, Godfrey, 30
Wilson, Monica, 30
Witwatersrand Native Labour Association (WNLA), 99, 102–3, 104, 105, 106, 107, 115
Wolpe, Harold, 7, 84
women: effects of male labor migration on, 16, 21, 36, 39, 62–81, 206 n. 18; exploitation of, 60–2, 204 n. 1, 205 n. 6; female-headed households, 55, 75, 77–8, 80–1, 171, 218 n. 61; and fertility, 86–7; as migrants, 42, 62, 78, 82–5, 131, 137, 145, 150–8; as workers, 144–5, 158–78; in pre-capitalist division of labor, 10–11; proletarianization of, 145–50
workers' counter-culture, 133–4

Xhosa, 154–5

Yoruba, 52–3, 70–1, 206 n. 27, 215 n. 18
'young men', 10, 12–14, 15–17, 24, 60–81, 82–5, 94

Zaire, 94, 101–3
Zambia, 30, 31, 48, 101, 102, 105, 106, 107, 108, 109, 110, 111, 112, 115, 131, 135, 136–8, 144, 153, 155–7, 159, 160, 163–4, 165–8, 174
Zanzibar, Zanzibar City, 124, 126
Zarma, 5, 198 n. 20
Zimbabwe, 35, 159, 174, 188, 205 n. 7
Zulu, 17, 63

The Politics of Africa's Economic Stagnation

RICHARD SANDBROOK

Director, Development Studies Programme, and Professor of Political Science at Scarborough College, University of Toronto

with JUDITH BARKER

African states are not, in any real sense, capitalist states. In post-colonial Africa one finds a form of neopatrimonialism – personal rule – that introduces a variety of economic irrationalities. This book analyses the social conditions impelling political adaptation and the consequences of personal rule for economic life, and surveys creative responses to the predicament African people now face.

The authors argue that personal rule is not simply a euphemism for ineptitude and mismanagement. They believe that it operates according to a particular rationality that shapes a ruler's actions when, in the absence of legitimate authority, he is confronted with the challenge of governing an unintegrated peasant society. Neopatrimonialism is essentially an adaptation of colonial-inspired political institutions to peculiar historical and social conditions, and this book focuses on the political factor as an important cause of Africa's economic ills.

Farm Labour

KEN SWINDELL

Senior Lecturer, Department of Geography, University of Birmingham

This book highlights the most important attributes of farm labour in Africa and places them within a context of historical change. International trade, colonialism, transport and the growth of towns have all exerted a powerful influence on rural Africa. More recently post-colonial states have attempted to reshape agriculture and transform rural societies. Yet agriculture is still dominated by small commodity producers who have retained control over their means of production, and it has not lost its labour-intensive character. Many small farmers now produce for local or international markets and this has been achieved by new patterns of work and labour organisation. Domestic production and family labour have been expanded or reduced by the spread of hired labour, as workers are redistributed between richer and poorer farmers and developed and underdeveloped regions. In addition, women have become more important as field labourers, as off-farm work for men becomes part of household reproduction.